SERVICE DESIGN AND TOURISM

CASE STUDIES OF APPLIED RESEARCH PROJECTS ON MOBILE ETHNOGRAPHY FOR TOURISM DESTINATIONS

— *Stickdorn & Frischhut (Eds.)*

Manufactured and published by Books on Demand GmbH, Norderstedt/Germany
Design: Quass von Deyen / Voss / Schneider GbR, Cologne/Germany
Layout by Jakob Schneider, Title design by Sylvia Niggeloh

ISBN 9783848216307

This publication is funded by the European Union under the CIP Competitiveness
and Innovation Program through the research project "Service design as an
approach to foster competitiveness and sustainability of European tourism".
The publication was presented during the 1st international conference on service
design and tourism, the SDT2012 in Innsbruck/Austria, August 23-24, 2012.

Bibliographic information published by the Deutsche Nationalbibliothek

The Deutsche Nationalbibliothek lists this publication in the Deutsche
Nationalbibliografie; detailed bibliographic data are available in the Internet at
http://dnb.dnb.de

SERVICE DESIGN AND TOURISM

CASE STUDIES OF APPLIED RESEARCH PROJECTS
ON MOBILE ETHNOGRAPHY FOR TOURISM DESTINATIONS

CONTENT

PREFACE

The field of design has changed completely during the past. Previously, design was seen as a profession that operates in specialist areas such as graphic design, product design, and fashion design; during the last 10 years it changed its scope from 'Design Centred Design' to 'User Centred Design'. As such, and building on the service-dominant logic and services marketing, service design goes beyond designing artefacts and is argued to be no longer limited to the design of tangible products only, but also designs complex and interactive service processes and ecosystems.

These developments lead to the emergence of 'service design', a multidisciplinary and systematic approach, which can cope with the functionality and complexity of services by visualizing their systems and processes as well as by placing the client at the heart of the process.

PREFACE

The aim of the research project "Service design as an approach to foster competitiveness and sustainability of European tourism" was to test the applicability of service design in the area of tourism. The tourism department at MCI Management Center Innsbruck was very proud to receive funding for a research project from the European Union under the CIP Competitiveness and Innovation Program and to be able to test the app myServiceFellow in seven pilot projects in selected European tourism destinations. The project successfully applied service design thinking to the tourism industry and particularly to prototype tourism-specific research methods, such as mobile ethnography.

We would like to thank the European Union for funding and technical support as well as for always being helpful with any question we addressed to them. This project could only be realised with the support of the pilot regions that were willing to apply a new innovative research method. The destination management organisations and service providers in the seven regions helped in establishing the contacts with tourists and provided the necessary support to conduct the pilot projects.

As the project lead partner we would like to thank all consortium partners for their professional engagement in the project and for the successful completion of the destination case studies. Furthermore we would like to congratulate the project team on this publication, which is a case sui generis.

Hubert Siller & Anita Zehrer
MCI Tourism

Consortium partners:
MCI Management Center Innsbruck, Austria (lead partner)
Linköping University, Sweden
Savonia University of Applied Sciences, Finland
SKEMA Business School, France
International Hotel School The Hague, Netherlands
Tourismuszukunft, Germany
AHO Design School of Oslo, Norway
Making Waves, Norway
Innovation Norway, Norway

Authors:
Marc Stickdorn, MCI Tourism
Birgit Frischhut, MCI Tourism
Josef Schmid, MCI Tourism
Stefan Holmid, Linköping University
Fabian Segelström, Linköping University
Tiina Kuosmanen, Savonia University of Applied Sciences
Pauli Verhelä, Savonia University of Applied Sciences
Frédéric Dimanche, SKEMA Business School
Girish Prayag, SKEMA Business School
Mady Keup, SKEMA Business School
Jan Huizing, Hotel School The Hague
Karoline Wiegerink, Hotel School The Hague
Danilo S. Huss, Hotel School The Hague
Rafaela Rotermund, Hotel School The Hague
Daniel Amersdorffer, Tourismuszukunft
Daniel Sukowski, Tourismuszukunft
Andrea Plesner, The Oslo school of Architecture and Design/Designit
Simon Clatworthy, The Oslo school of Architecture and Design
Arild Bjørn-Larsen, Making Waves

WHAT IS SERVICE DESIGN?

— Frédéric Dimanche, Mady Keup, Girish Prayag (1.1)
— Fabian Segelström, Stefan Holmid (1.2 - 1.4)

This chapter gives an introduction to service design. First, the importance of service experience is outlined. Second, historical roots of the disciplines are explained, followed by an overview of how a service design project is done and an introduction on the outcomes which can be expected from a service design project.

CHAPTER 1.1

THE SERVICE EXPERIENCE

Service experience is an important but difficult concept to define.

In the past, the service experience has been defined as a unique experience to an individual at a specific point in time, in a specific location, in the context of a specific event. More recently, the service experience has been viewed as both an individual and social experience. For example, a family weekend at a resort is both an individual and social experience that allows the family to bond. Also, service experiences often occur as a series of events that influence customer satisfaction and generally have an influence on consumer pre-purchase decisions, on-site evaluations, and post-purchase behaviour. Hence, the service experience cannot be considered as a static but rather dynamic process that is likely to evolve at different stages (e.g. from the pre-purchase to post-purchase stage) of experience consumption. This has been described as the 'process view' of the service experience suggesting that services are experienced in various stages or phases overtime. The experience often involves a transformation or change in customer behaviour due to learning experiences at each of the different stages.

The emotional side of service experiences

The service experience is often linked to outcomes such as service quality, perceived value and satisfaction, known as the 'outcome-based' service experience. According to this view, service experiences are associated with customers' evaluations of the service, preferences, moods and emotions. The consumer mainly assesses two components of quality: technical and functional. The former refers to what the customer actually receives from the service while the latter refers to the manner in which the service is delivered. Hence, managing the service experience is mainly concerned with quality issues and productivity. Far too often companies focus on the 'technical quality' but fail to understand and manage the true nature of customer satisfaction. Customer satisfaction is largely based on subjective personal reactions and feelings experienced by consumers at the time of the service delivery. Therefore, understanding affection and emotions remains an important part of the service experience. Perhaps more than any other service industry, tourism has the potential to elicit strong emotional and experiential reactions by consumers. In fact, tourism can elicit extraordinary experiences and the physical environment in which the service is delivered can trigger emotional and subjective reactions, too. Therefore, industry managers who use only service quality or service attributes to manage the service experience may not fully understand the true texture of the service experience. Ignoring the emotional side of service experiences may lead to an inaccurate understanding of customer perceptions and satisfaction as well as loyalty.

Service experiences are complex

The many facets of the service experience and the increasingly complex service environment characterized by connectivity of services and service performance management require service managers to develop service management strategies from a customers' point of view. The challenge lies in translating the service experience into manageable service encounters and service delivery as well as being able to specify the service environment that will most positively influence the customer. For example, the service experience is heavily affected by interactions with frontline staff (e.g. attitude towards customer, empathy and attentiveness) and the physical environment. Therefore, frontline staff requires appropriate training, empowerment, and clear job responsibilities to deliver the service experience promised to customers. Likewise, for the physical setting, service design and resourcing decisions are crucial management responsibilities. Increasingly, service organisations are using service (re)design for radical changes in service delivery. Managerial decisions are made with respect to how the interactions between customer and service provider will happen and how much of an impact this interaction will have on customer satisfaction. Also, by focusing on the customers' viewpoint of the service, organisations are able to understand how service experiences are constructed and remembered while also encouraging customers to actively participate in service design. This is perhaps why the service experience is described as the core of any service offering and can be facilitated by appropriate service design. The service experience remains a key concept of the service-dominant logic (S-D logic) which views the service experience as the basis of all business.

Service-dominant logic

An important aspect of the S-D logic is the co-creation of service experiences. According to this logic, on the supplier side, co-creation can be driven by service design innovation that enables the organisation to remain competitive. In the past, service providers were mainly adopting a service orientation to remain competitive. Service orientation can be viewed in two different ways. Service orientation occurs at the individual level whereby service employees are either service-oriented or not. The latter specifically considers internal service design characteristics and how the marketing strategy supports the organisation to become service oriented. In recent years, this concept of service orientation has evolved alongside the S-D logic. One major criticism of service orientation is that companies tend to be management-driven as opposed to customer driven in service design. On the contrary, the S-D logic suggests a commitment to collaborative processes with customers, service partners and employees. It is the holistic view of individuals (e.g. employees, customers, and other business partners) and organisations where collaboration creates synergy while service orientation takes more of a fragmentary approach to service design and management. The S-D logic offers integration of different perspectives to manage service and product experiences.

CHAPTER 1.2

ORIGINS OF SERVICE DESIGN

This chapter tells the story of how designers became interested in designing services and on how other service fields have inspired designers thinking about services.

Origins of design

Humans have always designed, but design as a profession is arguably a result of the industrial age. As production capability increased, producers needed to distinguish themselves from each other. One of the main ways this was done was through ornamentation. The ones who got the responsibility to do this were the early designers. However, designers soon realised they could contribute with more than just making things pretty – an early example of this is the Bauhaus movement.

These early designers focused on the use of the artefacts they designed, and how these artefacts were used. Ergonomics was an early influencer. As design continued to evolve during the 20th century, the focus on the humans who were going to use the artefacts increased. Designers started talking about users, and being user-centric in their work. The type of artefacts that became the focus of design kept growing, and with the introduction of computers and similar digital technology a whole new design area emerged – interaction design. Interaction design focuses on designing interfaces between technology and its users, and was inspired by the advances in user-centred design, in product/industrial design and other design fields.

Service design emerges

Service design emerged in the intersection between interaction design and product design, taking its inspiration from the user-centric practices of the two fields. Early service designers came from the various user-centric design disciplines and were driven by an insight that design could help in increasing the value for the customers to an even further degree by applying their thinking to services.

As service design has matured, the field had to face the inevitable question of what a service is. Thought inspiration came from the two closely interlinked fields of service management and service marketing. Those fields saw services as not-products – defining them based on the traits that differentiated services from products – but have now moved away from this view. Instead they argue that services are the basis of all economic transactions. Using the heading S-D logic, it is argued that people do not buy products and services just to have them but to achieve certain outcomes offered to them by the artefacts. The value offered by an artefact is thus what attracts customers. This value is always offered in a system of actions, interactions and artefacts. Every service is a system like this, and products are only one of the components of the service. This view of services as systems is central within service design as well, as reflected in the touchpoint concept that has become one of the central concepts in service design. Touchpoints are the parts of the service the customer interacts with, be it actions, interactions or products.

CHAPTER 1.3

TOOLS AND TECHNIQUES IN SERVICE DESIGN

How do designers design services? The main activities and tools associated with them are explained in this subchapter.

Introducing the service design process

Like all fields, service design comes with its own set of tools and techniques, some borrowed from other fields and some developed within the field. The overall design process is not very different in service design compared to other user-centred design (UCD) disciplines, but there are some specific challenges faced by service designers that are not faced by the traditional UCD-disciplines. These challenges are to a large extent connected to the increased complexity introduced by the idea of services as systems of touchpoints. Some of the main challenges faced by service designers involve how to represent the service in a good way and how to test (prototype) all aspects of the service system. These challenges have to a large part been solved by the introduction of new tools. The main steps in the service design process and some of the most common tools used in these stages can be seen in the following table (see the reading suggestions for an overview of these and more service design methods). As with all models the various stages appear more distinct than they are in reality. The move between various stages is a smooth natural process.

The service design process explained

To gather insights from various stakeholders (users, employees and more) is a crucial activity in service design projects and is usually the first thing a hired service designer will start planning. The most common approach is by employing some form of ethnographic method to gather insights – if possible the service designer will try to make sure to gather insights from the user in the use environment. This is usually done through a mixture of observations and interviews. The insights gathered in this phase will be the inspiration guiding work throughout the rest of the design process.

MAIN ACTIVITIES IN THE SERVICE DESIGN PROCESS AND MOST COMMON TECHNIQUES IN THE VARIOUS ACTIVITIES

Insights and inspiration	Ideation and refinement	Prototyping and evaluation	Finalisation and delivery
Benchmarking	Brainstorming	Bodystorming	Customer journeys
Ethnography	Co-creation workshops	Experience prototyping	Blueprints
Interviews		Enactment/Service walkthrough	Personas
Cultural probes			Business model canvas
Workshops		Desktop walkthrough	
Customer journeys			
Storyboards			
Touchpoint matrices			
Personas			

Having gathered stakeholder insights, the service designer faces one of the specific challenges for service design for the first time; how is a service represented in a good way? A series of different techniques have been developed by and applied to service design such as customer journeys, storyboards, blueprints and touchpoint matrixes. These techniques are commonly referred to as visualisations and are used to help articulate insights and solutions, to communicate the insights to the clients and as sources of inspiration as the design process continues.

The inspiration gathered will then serve as the basis for solidifying the ideas which the team wants to continue on. More often than not, several initial ideas will appear during the stakeholder research phase and they are brought into the ideation stage together with new ideas created during brainstorming sessions. Another common approach to ideation is co-creation, in which a group of different stakeholders are brought together in a workshop. In the workshop they are presented with insights from the service designers' research and are, with the help of various tricks, used in creating ideas for the service (that is, the service designer is more of a facilitator in this case). Whichever way ideas were formulated, the next step is to select and merge ideas in an iterative fashion to arrive at a small number of ideas to focus the attention and design work on.

As the ideas solidify, it is important to test that they do deliver on what the service should be offering (both from a provider and a customer perspective). This is done through the process of prototyping. Prototyping is a common technique within all UCD disciplines and is about building various types of models of the service system and/or its components to test that they fulfil their intended goals, and help in providing the customer with the desired value. The fact that services are systems consisting of several touchpoints poses some specific challenges to service designers.

Ideation and prototyping are highly iterative processes, insofar that the insights from the prototypes are used to further develop and refine the ideas. These new ideas are then made into new prototypes which are tested and the next iteration starts. As the changes from iteration to iteration become increasingly smaller, the service designer starts preparing the final deliverables of the service. Common ways of presenting the ideas are customer journeys, blueprints and prototypes. When new services are being developed, the business model canvas is rapidly growing in popularity as a communication tool.

CHAPTER 1.4

OUTCOMES OF SERVICE DESIGN PROJECTS

What can be expected by someone who hires a service designer? The strengths of using a service design approach are highlighted below.

The list of what you can expect from a service design process can be made long, and obviously is very case-dependent but there are two main themes which are re-occurring; a service offering which is competing on quality rather than price and a consistent service delivery across different channels (such as face-to-face, online and self-service). The suggestions for the new service are usually presented in a highly visual way; through customer journeys, blueprints and mock-ups of the envisioned service system.

As service designers aim at taking a holistic view of the service, they are often in a unique position to help their clients in making the service experience consistent across all different communication channels, be they face-to-face, digital or even self-service. These different channels are more often than not the responsibility of different individuals or even divisions of the service delivery company, leading to their development not being consistent. Bringing a holistic view will lead to a focus on improving the cross-channel experience, aiming at making sure that the customer's experience is good and leads to the same outcomes no matter which way the customer wants to interact with the service provider.

The user-centred nature of service design's roots has a strong focus on involving and designing for the humans in the service system. As there are humans involved on all sides of the service, it is crucial that the service designers get to understand all sides of the service so they can make well informed design choices. The service needs to make staff as well as customers happy to be successful. If given the opportunity to gain a full understanding of the service, the suggestions on the future design of the service made by the service designer will focus on all stakeholders.

By providing an improved service design, adopted to supporting the customer no matter how they choose to interact with the service and making sure the employees are happy in their work, service design led projects will aid you as a service provider in offering a service competing on quality and a great experience rather than on (lowest) price.

2

WHAT IS TOURISM?

— Frédéric Dimanche, Mady Keup, Girish Prayag

This chapter presents an overview of the tourism sector and discusses the importance of an experience-based approach to tourism management. First, it addresses tourism as a global phenomenon, presenting briefly key components of the tourism sector; second, it describes the various services or sub-sectors, retail and distribution of travel services, a key component of the service chain, and transportation.

Finally, the discussion moves on to what tourism is really about: creating experiences for tourists and visitors. This final part of the chapter, more academic, discusses the service experience and makes recommendations for managing this process to create quality and memorable tourist experiences.

CHAPTER 2.1

TOURISM – AN INDUSTRY THAT CREATES AND SELLS EXPERIENCES

Tourism is often considered to be the first economic sector in the world. Indeed, with a growth rate of about 4% per year.

According to the World Travel and Tourism Council (http://www.wttc.org), world travel and tourism continues to grow despite of international economic challenges that have affected the sector in the past 4 years. The following WTTC (2012) statistics are indicators of the on-going growth of tourism:

—— **Tourism's direct contribution** to GDP in 2011 was US$2 trillion and the industry generated 98 million jobs.

—— **Taking account** of its direct, indirect and induced impacts, travel and tourism's total contribution in 2011 was US$6.3 trillion in GDP, 255 million jobs, US$743 billion in investment and US$1.2 trillion in exports. This contribution represented 9% of GDP, 1 in 12 jobs, 5% of investment and 5% of exports.

—— **Growth forecasts** for 2012, although lower than anticipated a year ago, are still positive at 2.8% in terms of the industry's contribution to GDP.

—— **Long-term prospects** are even more positive with annual growth forecast to be 4.2% over the ten years to 2022.

In addition, the World Tourism Organisation (UNWTO) reported that international tourist arrivals grew by over 4% in 2011 to 982 million and forecasts a 2012 growth in tourist arrivals worldwide between 3 and 4%.

Defining tourism

"Tourism may be defined as the processes, activities and outcomes arising from the relationships and the interactions among tourists, tourism suppliers, host governments, host communities, and surrounding environments that are involved in the attracting and hosting of visitors" (Goeldner & Ritchie, 2006: 5). As a result, one can see that tourism involves numerous stakeholders that are all involved in the delivery of tourism-related services. The tourist is looking for psychological, social and physical experiences while suppliers are providing through their respective (but often combined or bundled) service opportunities for tourists to have those experiences. As part of the tourism system, one can identify around the tourists' natural resources and the environment, the cultural or built environment, government activities, and several operating sectors.

Those operating sectors make up what is often typically considered to be tourism. First, transportation appears to be central to tourism. Transportation services are of course essential in getting travellers from their homes to the target destination, but they are also critical in getting tourists to move within or between destinations, contributing to a dispersion of the impacts, be they positive or negative. Second, the accommodation sector, also very visible, includes numerous types of hostels, hotels, resorts, condominiums, campgrounds etc., as well as opportunities for travellers to stay in bed and breakfasts, farm houses and other private accommodation. Food services also contain numerous choices and great diversity for tourists, from gastronomic restaurants to cafeterias, fast food chain restaurants or hawker food stalls as well as caterers that provide services to groups. The attraction sector is composed of a vast variety of small businesses, museums, theme parks, natural, cultural, or historical attractions, as well as entertainment venues and shows (theatre and music on Broadway, etc.). Attractions are typically the reasons why leisure travellers visit a destination. Retail shopping is also an integral part of the visitor experience and can also be a primary reason for traveling. Often identified as part of, or closely related to the attraction sector, events beckon travellers because of their unique and special features. It may be a concert (an opera festival in Salzburg or Madonna on tour), a sport competition (the Olympics, a marathon, or a championship final), a professional show (ITB in Berlin or the International Film Festival in Cannes) or a convention, a cultural event (Mardi Gras in New Orleans or Oktoberfest in Munich). Finally, another important travel service sector is composed of retail travel agencies and tour operators. Retail and distribution as well as transportation will be further discussed later in this chapter.

Together, all the above-mentioned services contribute to create visitor experiences. Service design cannot only contribute to improving each individual service provider, but also, and perhaps more importantly, help each of the above services to liaise and to provide a seamless tourist experience. Certainly, we are not there yet, although recent progress in mobile technologies have contributed to offer new services that help create holistic experiences.

CHAPTER 2.2

RETAIL AND DISTRIBUTION

In the tourism context, distribution does not relate to the physical logistics (such as dispatch and storage) of tangible products to customers, but rather to the multiple roles of information dissemination, promotion, point of sale and product flow for tourism services. The example below may explain some of these factors in more detail.

In order to maximize profits, a hotel has to ensure optimization in its occupancy and rates for each trading day. Management therefore needs the hotel to be found and booked by its potential clients as easily as possible. Whereas promotional tactics such as digital marketing and advertising are aimed at raising the awareness of the hotel among its target markets, distribution channels, while they also enhance the promotional efforts, permit purchases (and therefore the flow of payments) from specific individuals or groups. It is important to bear in mind that services are perishable: unlike with physical goods, the hotel cannot store today's empty bedroom for sale tomorrow – the opportunity to sell has passed. The purchase, once made, is registered on the hotel's Computerized Reservation System and the guest receives a confirmation of purchase, either electronically (for an individual booking) or by contract (for a group or meeting booking).

Nature of distribution channels

Distribution channels can be direct (these belong to the company or organisation that is selling its tourism services) or indirect (a third party carries out distribution on behalf of the tourism service). An airline's reservation department, sales force and company website booking engine are examples of direct distribution. Here, the company is wholly responsible for the set up and staffing of its channels and their maintenance. Costs tend to be high, but the company maintains good control of brand communication and service to the customer.

It is in the best interest of the company/organisation to diversify its distribution channels in order to reach a maximum of potential customers. The tourism business therefore takes recourse to a host of indirect channels, from wholesaler or tour operator to retail travel agency. It is important to note that while the tourism supplier's market reach extends exponentially when using indirect channels, the main drawbacks are high costs (commissions etc.; see below), a lack of detailed control over service delivery and a potential loss of brand recognition.

Distribution is a highly competitive and potentially lucrative field and a great number of channels are fighting for the business of tourism suppliers who have to make an informed choice of which distributors to contract with on the guiding principles of cost, efficiency, market reach but also strategic fit.

Main intermediaries and business models

Third party distributors can also be called intermediaries who stand between the tourism suppliers and their end users. There are two principal types of distributors, the tour operator (TO) or wholesaler and the retail travel agency (TA).

The main differences between these two categories are as follows: (1) TOs buy products (tourism services such as transport, accommodation, visits to attractions etc.) in bulk, at discounted net prices from the supplier and then bundle these products into packages of differing duration, price and themes. They operate the "merchant model", where the distributor's profits come from including a margin on top of the total cost of the package. Typically, the end user or package tourist will not be aware of the isolated costs of individual elements. To the tourism supplier, the TO offers the opportunity to pre-sell a considerable amount of stock (hotel rooms or airline seats, for example). This can mitigate the perishability inherent in any tourism service. Although negotiation power of particularly large TOs (Thomas Cook and TUI are examples) may impose low net prices, their market reach will often compensate suppliers for this financial disadvantage. In addition, suppliers' own marketing expenses may be reduced if an important part of their stock has been contracted to a TO. (2) TAs, on the other hand, mostly operate as retailers on behalf of tourism suppliers or TOs. Whether from a bricks-and-mortar location or online, TAs have shop fronts that display a large variety of individual tourism services. Here travellers/tourists may be able to purchase just a ticket, hotel or rental car or bundle these items together in a tailor-made, dynamic package. They can also purchase already assembled TO packages. TAs are connected to suppliers' Computerized Reservation Systems through the so-called Global Distribution Systems, which permit instant verification, booking and updating of suppliers' available stock. As their remuneration, TAs receive a commission or percentage on services sold. The level of these commissions depends on the nature of the service, the agreement between TAs and suppliers and the market addressed. It is important to note that commission levels have been decreasing steadily over the last three decades to the point where certain categories of suppliers, such as airlines, will no longer pay the distributor. TAs have therefore begun to charge a service fee to the end customer.

To the tourism suppliers, retail TAs are congregators of businesses from independent travellers. By being implanted in specific catchment areas (including virtual presence with different language websites), TAs offer local market knowledge and support. Suppliers can also adjust remuneration levels to suit their objectives (such as selling stock in low season) and to reflect the relative strategic importance of the distributor. This is relevant to both leisure and business travel.

The role of the internet

Tourism distribution has experienced revolutionary changes since the use of electronic commerce has become widespread. According to ystats.com, a market research firm, "the share of the online segment compared to the total travel market is expected to increase to almost one third worldwide" in 2012.

The range of online third party distributors includes:

— **Online Travel Agencies** (OTA), which combine the TO and TA business models and include such giants as Expedia, Opodo and Orbitz.

— **Meta search sites** or fare aggregator sites, such as Cheapflights, Kayak.com or Roomkey.com. These allow end users to compare rates between different OTA and/or branded tourism supplier sites. These sites receive income from advertising and affiliate fees from the featured travel websites.

— **Social or group buying sites** such as Groupon or Living Social, which offer services and products at vastly reduced prices on the condition that a minimum number of buyers will make the purchase.

— **Private sales sites**, which ask users to register to receive so called flash sales offers that are greatly reduced in price, only open for a certain period of time and only to registered users. Examples are Tablet Hotels and JetSetter.

— **Opaque sales** work on the principle that individual tourism suppliers are not identified on the site until the purchaser has committed to their booking of, say, 'a four star resort hotel on the Côte d'Azur'. This allows suppliers to reduce their price when needing to dispose of stock quickly without doing visible damage to their brand.

Representation companies

For accommodation suppliers, specialist marketing consortia, such as Best Western or representation companies (Utell, Leading Hotels of the World etc.) can offer greater access to both travel intermediaries as well as end users. This is particularly useful for hotels that are not affiliated to a particular chain or want to promote themselves to a specific target segment that is addressed by the representation company. Cost to suppliers varies according to the required service level but typically consists of transaction fees and commission payable.

Service design

As pointed out earlier, distribution channels need to be evaluated not just in terms of cost or market and brand fit, but also in relation to service delivery to clients. This is true for direct channels but even more for third party distributors, even if online. It is important for tourism suppliers to achieve a good balance between increased efficiency and expected service levels.

CHAPTER 2.3
TRANSPORTATION

The personal car plays an important role in travel, particularly in North America and Europe. Statistics quoted by the US Travel Association state that "auto is the primary means of transportation used by leisure visitors (76%) who travelled for leisure purposes between August 2008 and July 2009".

However, travellers use a wide range of other transportation companies, depending on convenience, distance, cost, topographical access and duration of visit. Suppliers include airlines, coach, train, ferry and car rental companies, which will all be discussed further. In addition, this section also looks at cruise companies, even though it is possible to argue that their product is more extensive than mere transportation and could be considered to be part of the accommodation or even destination/resort sectors.

Airlines
Air travel can be chartered or scheduled flights. In the former, a TO, TA, or corporate buyer rents an aircraft or fleet for a specific route and duration. The flights may or may not operate, according to their load factor. Scheduled flights in contrast operate within the international airline network and companies have to respect flight slots, irrespective of load factor.

Scheduled airline companies are traditionally classified according to their operational and service level models. Distinction can be made between legacy carriers on the one hand, and budget airlines (or LCC, low cost carriers on the other: (1) Legacy airlines, also often called full service airlines, provide an extensive network of connections, either through their own routes or through so-called code sharing with alliance partners. They use the hub and spoke operation model, which consists in aggregating travellers originating from secondary destinations (the spokes) into a larger airport which serves as their base (or hub) in order to fly them to more distant destinations. They are responsible for synchronised passenger and luggage transfer, even when in transit. They also offer distinct upper, business and economy classes, with decreasing price structures and diminishing levels of service, from personalised attention, flat-bed seats and upscale menu options in first class to lesser legroom and limited catering in economy. (2) Low cost carriers operate short-haul, point-to-point routes, thereby achieving a cost reduction by not taking on board transfer and airline alliance costs. They also decrease aircraft purchase and maintenance costs by being able to restrict the type of aircraft they use to one or two main models. Other areas of economy are the use of secondary airports (with reduced handling charges) and a basic level of service that requires passengers to pay for all non-core transportation provision, such as on board catering, luggage check-in, priority boarding etc. These auxiliary services account for a considerable amount of LCC airline revenue, as is the case with EasyJet whose 2011 annual report shows that ancillary revenue contributed 20.8% (or GBP 719 million of total revenue).

Due to intense competition in short haul services, especially in North America, Europe and Asia, legacy airlines have increasingly adopted some of the low cost strategies within their business model (an example is reduced catering on board). Whether legacy or low cost, all airlines operate a strict revenue management strategy on pricing, whereby prices increase in line with a rise in demand and a reduction in available capacity on the route (load factor).

Train travel

Travelling by train has been an established feature of European leisure tourism in particular. Europe, however, is not the only region to feature rail transportation. Amtrak in the United States "travels to over 500 destinations in 46 states" (www.amtrak.com), while in China the government is actively developing extensive infrastructure to serve a nation-wide express train network. It is important to note that even though most of the world's rail network is managed by the public sector, there has been widespread recent private sector investment, particularly in the rolling stock (trains) and some routes have been partly or wholly privatized. This is the case, for example of Eurostar, the service linking London and Ashford in England with Lille and Paris in France and Brussels in Belgium. Some rail routes, such as the Trans-Siberian Railway and the Blue Train in South Africa have become tourism experiences in their own right rather than mere means of transportation.

Coaches

In a similar vein to train networks, coach companies such as the Greyhound Lines in North America and Australia and Eurolines in Europe link major city centres to each other and depart at specific time slots (schedules).

Car Rental companies

Often used in combination with flights (so-called fly & drive), car rentals permit travellers to hire vehicles for a certain duration. Well-known car rental companies are Hertz, Avis, Europcar and Sixt.

Rental of recreational vehicles (RVs) is also popular in many destinations that invite visitors to explore further flung parts of the country, for example New Zealand or the USA.

Ferry companies

Ferries transport travellers between the mainland and surrounding islands, such as the ferries in Greece, departing from Piraeus in Athens to the Aegean islands. Apart from transportation tickets, ferries also achieve revenue through catering, accommodation, gaming and spa and fitness services on board.

Cruise companies

Cruise liners transcend the sphere of mere transportation – they have in fact been described as "floating holiday resorts" (Holloway & Taylor, 2006: 353). On board they offer a range of cabin accommodation and of restaurants, entertainment, casinos, spa and fitness facilities and, on specialist cruises, thematic activities such as archaeology, history, cookery and wine appreciation, etc. Prices vary according to season of travel, size and location of cabin, crew to passenger ratio, distance and duration of stay on board. Cruise ships derive additional revenue from onshore excursions, spa treatments and other non-included consumptions, such as à la carte gourmet dinners and a superior drinks selection. While the biggest cruise ships to date, Royal Caribbean-owned Oasis of the Seas and Allure of the Seas carry over 6.000 passengers, cruise ships can be of differing size, depending on where they are deployed. There are river cruises, coastal cruises and ocean going cruises. Major cruise locations are the Caribbean, the Mediterranean, the Arab Gulf, the Baltic Sea, Norway, Alaska and Antarctica.

Service design

All transportation suppliers benefit from paying close attention to service design, for varying reasons. While it might be to increase service quality of the service in the upper classes of airlines or the luxury cruises, it could also be to improve efficiency in the rapid turnaround of aircraft for low cost carriers.

Following this discussion of tourism and of some of its key sectors, the following section focuses on the tourist experience, or more specifically, the service experience in tourism. It makes recommendations for service management and more particularly, argues that tourism management and marketing practices should be experience-based.

3

DESIGNING TOURISM SERVICES

— Girish Prayag, Frédéric Dimanche, Mady Keup (3.1 – 3.2)
— Marc Stickdorn (3.3)

"If you cannot measure it, you cannot manage it" is a common saying in business. Management comprises planning, organising, leading, and controlling an organisation or effort. Is it possible to manage experiences in tourism?

This chapter describes various approaches to understand the complexity of tourism experiences. Moreover, it recaps different attempts to design and measure tourism experiences and discusses why even entrepreneurs of the tourism industry can benefit from service design thinking.

CHAPTER 3.1

THE TOURISM EXPERIENCE

Although many concepts associated with service experience such as the S-D logic, service blueprint, theatrical methods, and service mapping are used in the tourism industry; the tourism experience is very distinct from the service experience and other types of customer experiences.

The secret to a good customer experience is not the multiplicity of features on offer, but how customer value is embedded in each feature. Despite the tourism sector being driven by customer experiences, it is hard to identify the components of the tourism experience. The components are not necessarily the same as those of the service experience. Some researchers suggest that the tourism experience is a very subjective and personalised experience, often influenced by society, culture and different economic systems. Therefore, the tourism experience is distinct from other 'types' of experiences for many reasons such as tourists are diverse, trips are of various types, and the content of the tourism experience changes and evolves more radically compared to other service industries. Also, the tourism experience is often linked to other customer or service experiences. Thus, understanding the tourism experience requires different theoretical approaches to be used. For example, the tourist experience includes various components that can provide emotional, physical, intellectual and even spiritual fulfilment. Therefore disciplines such as marketing or management alone, cannot fully explain the tourist experience. Over the years two main schools of thoughts have emerged to understand the tourism experience: social science and marketing/management.

The social science approach

As part of the social science approach, early conceptualisations of the tourism experience emphasize the tourism experience as a distinct experience from everyday life. According to this view, tourists mainly travelled in search of strangeness and novelty, or simply to experience change. Hence, the tourism experience often begins with the 'ordinary' (e.g. taxi to the airport), progresses into the 'heightened' moments (e.g. visiting the Great Canyon), and returns to the 'ordinary' (e.g. flight to home-country), suggesting that temporality is central to the experience. The term 'tourist gaze' is used to describe the process through which a tourist visualises and interprets the destination that he or she visits. Since the 90s this idea has been challenged by many with an overwhelming conclusion that the distinction between everyday life and tourist experiences is disappearing due to media and technology. Tourists can enjoy destination attractions via video and virtual reality displays within the comfort of their own home. Experiences once confined to tourism are currently accessible in various contexts of everyday life. Different kinds of people may also desire different forms of the tourism experience. For example, five common experience forms are: recreationary (e.g. entertainment), diversionary (e.g. recharging energy), experimental (e.g. rediscovering oneself), experiential (e.g. staged authenticity) and existential (e.g. ultimate nostalgia). Tourists searching for profound meanings (e.g. nostalgia) in their travel experiences, for example, would conform to the 'experiential' or 'existential' forms of the tourist experiences. Basically, the social science approach regards the tourism experience as a form of peak experience.

The marketing/management approach

The marketing/management approach treats the tourism experience as consumer or service experience. This experience can be differentiated at two levels: (1) the degree of customer involvement (passive vs. active participation) in the experience and (2) the desire of the customer to connect or engage with the experience (absorption vs. immersion). The four types of experiences that emerge out of these two levels are: (i) entertainment (passive-absorption) as in the case of music concerts; (ii) educational (active-absorption) as in the case of sports practice; (iii) escapist (active-immersion) as in the case of working holidays or mass tourism in exotic locations and; (iv) aesthetic (passive-immersion) such as in sightseeing, trekking and snorkelling while on holidays. According to this view, through the experience the tourist is able to reach a 'sweet spot' similar to the 'peak' experience described in the social science approach. A tourist destination should therefore be able to deliver experiences at all four levels, although these levels may be emphasized differently for each targeted segment of visitors.

The total customer experience

Additionally, for destinations to differentiate their experience from other competing places, they have to develop visitor's emotional attachment with the place and
a brand community. This can be achieved by engineering the 'total customer experience' (TCE) and lasting customer loyalty (LCL) that enable companies to main-
tain their customer focus and create customer preferences. TCE can be seen in Disney's theme parks with its hundreds of engineered cues that are all coordinated
and networked to generate a mix of excitement, entertainment and adventure.
TCE has been defined as a "totally positive, engaging, enduring, and socially fulfilling physical and emotional customer experience across all major levels of one's
value chain and one that is brought by a distinct market offering that calls for active interaction between consumers and providers" (Mascarenhas et al., 2006: 399).
It is based on six main principles.

——— **Principle 1:** Anticipating and fulfilling customer needs and wants
better than competitors

——— **Principle 2:** Providing real consumer experiences that
competitors cannot match

——— **Principle 3:** Providing real emotional experiences that go beyond
the physical attributes of the product/service

——— **Principle 4:** Experiences as distinct market offerings

——— **Principle 5:** Experiences as interactions

——— **Principle 6:** Experiences as engaging memories

TCE offers a great way for service augmentation given that the experience is created by the active involvement and interaction between the service provider and
the customer. The customer cherishes such an enduring experience before, during and long after service delivery. The stages described above are similar to those
described earlier for the service experience. In tourism, these stages have been
specifically described as anticipation of travel, experience at the destination and
reflection on the travel experience post visit. However, the activities and decision-
making processes involved in a traditional product-centred experience (e.g. buying a washing machine), service-centred experience (e.g. a flight) and the tourism

experience at each of these stages vary considerably. This perhaps explains why both the social science and marketing/management approach to understanding the tourism experience have been criticized.

The complexity of the tourism experience

Specifically, the social science approach fails to consider the influence of supporting experiences such as eating and sleeping on the tourism experience. Without the supporting experiences, the peak experience cannot happen. More importantly, if failure points occur with the supporting experiences, the TCE can be jeopardized no matter how strong the peak experience is. In the marketing/management approach, the supporting experiences are included as being able to influence the tourism experience, but this approach considers the tourism experience as very similar to other forms of customer experiences. There is no explicit differentiation between the service and tourism experience, often treating the tourism experience as being exclusively about service quality. The marketing/management approach also eludes the fact that supporting consumer experiences (e.g. eating out in restaurants) can also generate peak experiences as in the case of culinary tourism. The S-D logic described earlier incorporates some of these limitations by emphasizing the importance of service design for managing customer experiences holistically and the customer as a co-producer. Yet, the S-D logic fails to consider that services are dynamic experiences and co-constructed with consumers according to their expectations and perceptions. Some customers may or may not want to actively participate in the co-creation process but they nevertheless experience the service regardless of whether the quality of the experience is below their expectations. This phenomenon is inherent to the tourism experience where some are more involved and actively participate in shaping their destination experience (e.g. backpackers) while others are more passive observant/participants (e.g. packaged tours).

In addition, the tourism experience is increasingly facilitated by media and technology. The tourist also actively attempts to facilitate and/or interpret the tourism experience of another individual. For example, the tourist guide is a well-known facilitator of the tourist experience responsible for linking tourists to attractions, facilities and hosts. These facilitators also known as 'mediators' of the tourism experience not only exist at the experiential phase of the visit (i.e. on site) but also at the pre-travel stage (i.e. vacation planning) and the post-travel stage (i.e. recollection). Increasingly, technology based mediators such as the internet, mobile phones, and digital cameras are used by tourists at all stages of the tourism experience. This phenomenon suggests a shift from the 'tourist gaze' to a 'mobilised virtual gaze' that enables people to travel mentally and emotionally (i.e. experience tourism activities) without moving physically to the destination. The tourism experience has also become more complex due to service providers such as destination marketers making available features such as images, vodcasts, podcasts and blogs on their websites to better support the tourist experience at all stages. These advances allow tourists to benefit from being able to use multimedia features such as text, images, video streaming and virtual reality to enhance and add value to their tourism experiences.

Limitations in capturing the tourism experience

Due to the complexity of the tourism experience described above, this experience cannot be treated as similar to other customer or service experiences. In fact, customer and service experiences are only components of the tourism experience. Also, existing ways of researching the tourist experience do not fully capture the 'mobilised virtual gaze'. Therefore, it is questionable whether existing theoretical approaches such as the S-D logic can be fully applied to tourism and tools such as the TCE can be used effectively to explain the tourism experience. The increasing recognition of the symbolic and emotional values of the tourism product and the fact that tourists may engage in different modes of experiences within the same trip (e.g. nostalgia and experimental when visiting a heritage site) or one mode of experience over multiple trips (e.g. diversionary for spa and wellness products), suggest that existing models/frameworks have limitations in capturing the tourism experience and its linkages with the service experience and other forms of customer experiences. Also, the tourism experience is sensitive to socio-demographics such as age and gender as well as to cultural diversity. The way in which Chinese tourists, for example, engage with service provision in Europe is not necessarily the same compared to Western tourists. Consequently, a more holistic approach is necessary to understand and manage tourism experiences.

CHAPTER 3.2

MANAGEMENT OF THE TOURISM EXPERIENCE

Management of the tourism experience can be facilitated by identifying: (i) peak tourism experiences; (ii) supporting consumer experiences and; (iii) daily routine experiences.

Recognizing the interchangeability and differentiation of peak and supporting experiences by tourists, for example, allows better understanding of the tourism experience. That is, some components of the supporting consumer experiences such as the accommodation (e.g. a 5-star hotel) and local cuisine can turn into peak experiences. Likewise, peak experiences such as the beach can turn into a supporting consumer experience, if for example the backpacker has an unplanned romantic encounter on the beach. Also, recognizing that peak and supporting experiences are in sharp contrast to daily routine experiences but remain an extension of the daily experience in an intensified form, allow better categorization of experiences into 'ordinary' vs. 'extraordinary', 'routine' vs. 'unusual', and 'the familiar' vs. 'novel'. In this way the components of the tourism experience can be identified and hence better managed. However, this approach neither highlights the difficulties in measuring the experience (e.g. what is considered as an extraordinary experience?) nor how to design the tourism experience for better delivery of the experience.

Measuring the tourism experience

Increasingly, consumers are looking for a combination of affective memories, sensation and symbolism in their tourism experience to create a holistic long-lasting personal experience. This is a core philosophy of the experience economy. Yet, a common criticism of the experience economy is the inability for managers to measure consumer experiences using identifiable components that are valid across product/service categories. In tourism in particular, everything tourists go through at a destination can be considered as an experience, be it behaviour or perception, or a cognitive or emotional experience. The difficulties associated with the measurement of the tourism experience have impeded the development of effective ways or processes to manage this experience. Tourists are generally concerned with the experience of visiting, seeing, learning, enjoying and living in a different mode of life when travelling and therefore these could potentially be the focus of measurement. Likewise, given tourists desire to actively engage in creating experiences instead of passively seeing, watching, and/or learning about artefacts, history, and exhibits, measuring their level of involvement is another important aspect. Some researchers suggest measuring the experiential dimensions of education, entertainment, aesthetics and escapism. Specifically, learning, enjoyment and escape are inherent in many tourist activities such as a bed and breakfast stay or cruise experience, suggesting that measurement should include also supporting services. These experiential dimensions influence satisfaction and repeat visitation differently and therefore understanding how they can be managed is of critical importance to service providers and destination marketers.

Designing the tourism experience

If the tourism experience is more difficult to define and measure, how can it be designed to facilitate its management? Anecdotal evidence exists on how to design a good tourism experience. For example, good design makes the most routine (e.g. check-in at the hotel) and the weightiest customer experiences (e.g. diving with dolphins) pleasant and efficient, and allows customers to reach the 'sweet spot' or 'peak experience'. The various service design principles suggested include: (i) segmenting the pleasurable components of the service into identifiable chunks; and (ii) try to combine unpleasant processes into a singular 'get it over' activity. Customers are less likely to complain about service quality when they have control over some part of it as suggested by the S-D logic. Service experiences should thus be designed in such a way as to engage all the five senses. The deliberate design and execution of service experiences as a distinctive management discipline with its own principles, tools, and techniques is a new domain of research and remains unexplored in the tourism industry.

Designing experience-centric services

The term 'experience design' is used to describe the development of experience-centric services with the end goal of engaging customers in such a way that it builds emotional connections (Zomerdijk & Voss, 2010). A number of ways to design experience-centric services exist such as:

—— **Designing a series of service encounters** and cues and also orchestration of these cues that occur at different points in time and space. This approach is similar to the concept of service blueprint and the service experience blueprint (SEB) described earlier.

—— **Involving sensory design.** The physical environment can be designed to evoke particular emotions and responses. The traditional way of managing the tourist experience has often ignored the influence of a variety of sens-escapes such as soundscapes, smellscapes, and tastescapes by privileging the visualscape or tourist gaze. In the experience economy, the experiential marketing framework highlights the importance of managing the sensory alongside the affective, intellectual, behavioural and social dimensions of the consumer experience.

—— **Engaging customers.** This can be done by a process of co-creation described earlier. It is also important to establish rapport, empathy, feelings of care and friendliness between service providers and customers during the service encounter. It involves the conveying of authentic understanding, which is particularly important in extended, affective, and intimate service encounters. Authentic understanding is achieved when service providers and customers engage in self-revelation, use emotional energy, and connect as individuals rather than simply performing their respective roles.

—— **Dramatic structuration.** This is similar to the theatre metaphor described earlier, where every component of the service encounter has to be scripted and engineered to enhance the customer's experience and recollection of it.

—— **Fellow customers.** The presence of other customers and significant others such as family, friends and colleagues have an inherent ability to impact either positively or negatively on the service experience. For example, crowding and unruly behaviour of fellow customers normally have a negative impact while opportunities to socialise or bond with fellow customers enhance the service experience. A possible way of addressing the value of fellow customers is to establish a brand community that stimulates customers to share their ownership or consumption experience.

—— **Backstage services.** Service provision inherently has two parts, the frontstage (e.g. the hotel lobby) and the backstage (e.g. the kitchen). Isolating the backstage from the frontstage to maximize efficiency or operational excellence is likely to result in coordination problems that may damage the frontstage experience. Backstage work should not be treated as a separate entity; rather it should be characterized by a close connection with and its devotion as a supporting role to front stage. Back office employees help create the contextual elements of an experience and hence are part of the experience (Zomerdijk & Voss, 2010).

Using these processes managers should pay attention to: (i) pre and post purchase behaviours; (ii) physical aspects of the customer journey and; (iii) emotional aspects of the customer journey. Thus, by carefully adapting these stages, designing tourist journeys and applying other design principles, service providers in the tourism industry may improve tourism experiences and better engage their customers.

Customer experience modelling

Other authors propose the use of customer experience modelling (CEM) to represent and systematize the customer experience, in an effort to guide service design efforts. CEM provides a modelling tool that enables a manageable abstraction of the complex service reality and facilitates creativity in the service design process. It supports a holistic view of customer experiences and explicitly considers the physical elements, the technology-enabled systems, and the actors involved in each activity throughout the customer journey. CEM does not substitute for existing methods, but provides a higher-level approach that systematizes experience information to support the early stages of service design (Teixeira et al., 2012). CEM adapts concepts such as human activity modelling (HAM), customer experience requirements (CER), multi-level service design (MSD) in the modelling process. The applicability of this tool on tourism experience design has yet to be evaluated.

Designing destination experiences

Today, how to design destination experiences both at a macro (e.g. country) and micro (e.g. city) level remains enigmatic. Experience has always existed in destinations given that a destination consists mostly of a bundle of services such as transportation, accommodation and attractions, and these often represent the core or supporting services of the tourism experience. Hence, the competitiveness of a tourist destination is largely dependent on the quality of experiences associated with its core and supporting services. However, for years it was taken for granted that the experience is a by-product of the destination, rather than created, developed and innovated. In particular, the application of service design for tourist destinations requires a holistic analysis of all sequencing touchpoints between customers and service providers within a complex tourism product and collecting data about customer experiences at 'touchpoints'. Touchpoints are described as instances of direct contact of the customer with the service itself or with representations of it by the company or some other third party. The term 'customer corridor' is often used to portray the series of touchpoints that a customer experiences. Not all touchpoints are of equivalent value. Also, the analysis of customer experiences requires extending touchpoints beyond the actual service period to include also pre- and post-service periods. In this way, tourism and destination managers can have a holistic view of their product/services thereby facilitating (re)design, intentionally produced, organized, foreseen, calculated, priced and explicitly charged for if necessary (Stamboulis & Skayannis, 2003).

Service design becomes a core strategic concern in creating and adding value to the tourism experience

Once designed, the service experience of tourists has to be managed and the performance evaluated. At the destination level, experience management if neglected tends to focus on service provision only. Traditionally, principles of experience-based management has drawn from the manufacturing/service sector with a focus on translating managerial inputs into outputs which are subjectively experienced by participants. Gradually, this approach has been replaced by activity based management where the provision of activity opportunities represented managerial end products. In tourism, a benefit-based management system has more relevance given its ability to describe the experience-based management outputs more explicitly, linking activities, settings, experiences, and benefits in a sequence. This system focuses on service settings, through which experiences are facilitated, and the extent to which these settings are contrived implicitly or explicitly. In particular, it is necessary to ask questions regarding the range of experiences within a setting, how types of tourists should be identified best, and how the experiences may be facilitated. Yet, the bottom line is that customer experience does not improve until it becomes a top priority in the organisation and work processes, and until systems and structures change to reflect that. This is the most effective way to create engaging and lasting experiences for customers. Disney for example has a holistic approach to TCE where every adventure, every Disney character, every employee, every shop, and even the long waiting lines systematically manage positive sensory and emotional experience in a commercial setting.

At a tourist destination, the moments of truth are many, and the customer has the possibility of arranging these moments or touchpoints in different ways. Visitors also have the possibility to define which touchpoints are notable and which ones they would ignore or overlook. Also, customers are 'movement-driven,' that is, they are constantly moving at destinations and between destinations. They have access to multiple technologies of travel and communication that move ideas, information, people, images and objects across varying distances. Therefore, experience-based tourism management strategies should involve strategies to manage the setting, strategies to manage the people involved in the setting, the story that the experience managers want to communicate, and the use of technology to enhance the experience. In fact, tourism experience management is about creating a story about the destination and the task of informing and steering the innovation and creativity process that leads to the creation of new themes of experience related to the overall story. Contrary to conventional tourism that exploits inflexible assets such as nature and infrastructure, experience-based management of tourism seeks to exploit the intangible assets of the destination (Stamboulis & Skayannis, 2003).

CHAPTER 3.3

WHY TOURISM NEEDS SERVICE DESIGN

Researchers identified the numerous tourism entrepreneurs as one of the main drivers for innovation and the creation of outstanding tourism experiences.

Tourism entrepreneurs are people who, "through a combination of perceptiveness, creativity and the fortuitous confluence of events, are constantly identifying opportunities as they arise and creating the organisations to pursue them" (Russel & Faulkner, 2004: 557). The idea of an iterative innovation process according to a service design process is far from new for tourism entrepreneurs. These entrepreneurs have been the pioneers in the development of tourism services and they apply basic principles of service design thinking every day:

—— **Hands-on insights** when hoteliers work along with their employees – from frontline staff to the backoffice.

—— **Contextual interviews** with customers – every time they sit together at the hotel bar.

—— **Empowering** their staff to develop new ideas and solutions.

—— **Constant evaluation** and re-thinking of existing processes from a customer perspective.

—— **Adapting best-practices** and solutions from outside the industry.

However, innovation processes are often intuitive and not built on a strategic design process due to the fact that the tourism industry is dominated by small and medium sized enterprises (SMEs). 94% of European tourism companies have less than six employees. Such a fragmented industry involves both challenges and opportunities for business since SMEs have to cope with limited budgets for product development and advertising. However, on the other hand SMEs also have corporate responsibility and flat organisational structures – both ideal conditions for innovation.

Marketing shifts from advertisements to genuine experiences.
Memories of outstanding tourism experiences generate word-of-mouth, which nowadays has enormous reach through social media and tourism review websites. In particular the latter has an impact on the industry that cannot be stressed enough. Tourism products underlie a unique buying decision process, since most customers decide and often pay months in advance – and in the case of leisure tourism invest not only money, but their precious holidays. In this decision process, trust towards tourism brands and their products is most important. Tourism companies attempt to convince guests of a certain service quality standard through strong brands or quality labels. Tourists nowadays trust first and foremost other guests' experiences though. A recent study of German tourists shows that significantly more guests trust the opinions of other customers than any corporate communications. 95% consider online customer reviews as trustworthy and 65% would no longer book any travel without previously checking customer reviews on respective websites (IUBH, 2011). Through this apparent increase in transparency of tourism offerings, marketing strategies need to shift from classical advertisements to genuine experiences. It's the individual guest's experience that makes or breaks a successful tourism product.

Destinations as complex service ecosystems
Tourism products are bundles of various services. A leisure holiday involves a variety of different services, which are often provided by several companies: The travel to the destination, local transportation, accommodation, gastronomy, and leisure activities, to name but a few. Tourists, however, evaluate the whole experi-

ence within a destination, which makes tourism products particularly challenging to design. Even if the task is to design a single service for one provider, a complex service ecosystem needs to be taken into consideration. This consists not only of stakeholders of the service on hand, but also the whole ecosystem a customer experiences within a certain destination. A destination is a geographic area that the respective visitor selects as a travel destination. It encompasses all necessary amenities for a stay, including accommodation, catering, entertainment, and activities. It is therefore the actual competitive unit within incoming tourism which must be run as a strategic business unit (Bieger, 2005). Although there are also destinations, which are centrally managed and owned by one company, such as theme parks or resorts, most destinations consist of a fragmented system of companies and actors. However, ultimately it is the tourist who defines a destination and as a rule-of-thumb, the perceived size of a destination increases with the distance tourists travel. The unique buying decision process of tourists includes another characteristic regarding its gradual set of choice. The decision for a destination involves various alternatives beyond obvious competitors: Tourists chose between city, sun and beach or mountain destinations in every season of the year, which makes it hard if not even impossible for destinations to know their direct competitors. An authentic destination identity across all involved stakeholders leads to a consistent destination image in the tourists' minds. This clear image is crucial for a profound decision in the tourists' buying process, but on the other hand demands a high level of cooperation between the destination's stakeholders. The concept of destination personality – comparable to a description of a destination as a persona – supports stakeholders to find a common viewpoint and understand their destination image from a customer's point of view. Following the buying decision process during the next set of tourist's choices, many of the very same stakeholders are competitors and as such need to differentiate from each other within the destination. This leads to a classic prisoners' dilemma and in fact represents one of the main challenges of destination management. At the same time, this is one of the biggest future opportunities for service design in tourism. Service design thinking provides processes and methods to create organisational structures and understand the culture required to deliver superior customer experiences within a complex ecosystem of both public and private organisations such as tourism destinations. Design research approaches like ethnographic research, storytelling, mapping customer journeys and stakeholder value networks are invaluable tools for destination management.

IN SEARCH FOR AUTHENTIC USER INSIGHTS

— *Pauli Verhelä (4.1 – 4.2)*
— *Marc Stickdorn (4.3)*

Design research has shown that the role of design has changed and today the object of design is more concentrated on creating service systems instead of individual products or artefacts. Design requires a deep understanding and interpretation of the needs and motivations of users. Moreover, it also involves various stakeholders who contribute to the process by advancing their expertise in facilitating co-operation and co-create new solutions to the users' problems. Design today can work as a social agent and be in a role of explaining practises in people's daily life.

CHAPTER 4.1
ETHNOGRAPHY

Ethnography has its origins and disciplinary home in cultural anthropology. The focus of ethnography is the interpretation of cultural groups or phenomena. Ethnographic research aims to produce knowledge, which is difficult to retrieve by inquiries or surveys. Usually, the research topics are everyday routines, considered as trivial or self-evident and which people do not consciously think about. The topics might also be issues that people are not able to speak about or which do not come into their minds in traditional interview situations.

In an ethnographic research the ethnographer gets under the skin of the phenomenon, target group or target society that he or she is researching. The key issue for a researcher in the study field is to get close enough to the target society and to analyse the findings focusing on cultural practices or socio-cultural patterns of action and describing how culture simultaneously constructs and is formulated by people's behaviour and experiences.

The methods of ethnography are observing or participant observing, interview and content analysis of artefacts and documents.

—— **Observing** means that 1) daily tasks and practices, 2) interaction and verbal or non-verbal communication between people, 3) material and spatial arrangements and 4) different artefacts e.g. pictures, documents and various articles and use of them are observed from outside and recorded in the examined society of place by the researcher.

—— **In participant observing** the researcher is participating in the daily life of the target society and tries to be a member of the group in order to be deeply engaged in everyday practices of the group to get an insider's perspective and use his own persona as a research-instrument. The roles of participant observations are defined according to the depth of participation in the society: 1) A complete participant is a full, inside member of the target society. 2) A participant-as-observer is a participant of the daily life, who observes it from an outsider's viewpoint. 3) An observer is an outsider who is partly participating in the everyday life of the group and 4) A complete observer is an outsider who does not have any deep participatory role in the group.

An interview in ethnography is less formal and less interviewer-driven than normal types of interviews. Regardless of the level of participation and form of interview the main thing in ethnographic research is 'being there' as David Fetterman (1989: 19) states: 'asking questions, seemingly stupid, yet insightful questions, observing and writing down what is seen or heard'. Key issue is that all the beliefs, practices and other everyday features of the target group's culture are always inseparable from the certain context and must be described and interpreted within the framework of the social group's view of reality.

The classical ethnographies were more or less anthropological studies about foreign cultures, usually far away outside of the western world and conducted by western researchers. Contemporary research is mostly 'home-based' e.g. researches of functions of an organisation or company, mystery shopping to describe how service processes are meeting with the quality requirements, auto-ethnographies or studies of oneself or netnographies (virtual ethnographies), which are conducted in the virtual world.

CHAPTER 4.2

MOBILE ETHNOGRAPHY

Ethnography is used within many social sciences and has spread in many design disciplines with all disciplines sharing a strong focus on the experience of people in their own context during all stages of the service delivery process.

What is mobile ethnography?

A weakness in ethnographic studies based on observation of people's behavioural interaction with services is that they do not immediately yield data that can be analysed. Furthermore, considering the complexity of tourism products regarding temporal and spacial dimensions, these methods permit only fragmentary exploration or involve enormous costs in terms of time and resources. Therefore, for the tourism industry, mobile ethnography becomes of interest, which can be described as geographically independent ethnographic research for a specific subject matter, such as tourism products or destinations. The proceeding dispersion of smartphones, such as iPhones and respective apps, provides a new opportunity to gather time and location independent user-centred information. Such a user-centred approach must keep the user's view in mind and argues for the user as an integral, participatory force in the service process.

The development of mobile ethnography

Mobile ethnography means a process where researchers collect information using ethnographic methods in a modern way. Where classical ethnographers travelled to distant locations to participate in the target society's everyday life to gather the data for their research, modern ethnographies use modern technology to get under the skin of the target group or person and to transfer the collected data. The early devices used in mobile ethnography were cameras, video recorders and today the technology provides the researchers with laptops, iPhones, iPads and other similar mobile appliances through which the target group can describe, scan, record and send their insights to the researcher using specially designed programs and applications. Mobile ethnography makes it possible to get direct user information which is not just recalling experiences and giving feedback to them afterwards, but reporting experiences online at the time of the experience, on the very spot or location of the experience and in the mental space of the experience itself based on the genuine feelings generated by the experiences.

Mobile ethnography and user-centred design

Mobile ethnography follows the principal ideas and methods of user-centred design. User-centred design was used as a term describing a new approach in product development in the 1980s. The term refers to the influence of end-users in a development process that includes the recommendation of placing the end-users into the centre of the design process. First implementations took place in the ICT–development but soon the approach was adapted also to other areas of service production. The terms defining users are: 1) Primary users are the ones who actually use services and products. 2) Secondary users are the ones who occasionally use the product or service and 3) Tertiary users are the ones who somehow are affected by the use of the product or service or they are the ones who make the decision of procurement of it. The experiences and opinions of all these types of users plus other significant stakeholders should be taken into consideration in the development process.

CHAPTER 4.3
MYSERVICEFELLOW

MyServiceFellow is the result of multiple publicly-funded research projects and is one of the first prototypes of a mobile ethnography app. The app enables customers to capture touchpoints by themselves right in the moment of an experience.

MyServiceFellow

MyServiceFellow allows adding and assessing touchpoints on a 5-point Likert scale and documents these touchpoints with text, audio, photos or videos, which can be each individually flagged as positive or negative to reflect different aspects of each touchpoint. Participants can download myServiceFellow to their smartphones (i.e. Android phones, iPhone, iPad, iPod Touch, etc.) from the Android Market Place or the AppStore and map their individual customer journey, e.g. from the pre-service period when booking the holiday, gaining information about the destination and travelling to the destination as well as during the service-period in a respective destination and in the post-service period when customers share their experiences on- and offline. The caption of date, time and GPS data of each touchpoint allows the construction of a customer journey based on either route or time sequence of the user even for complex tourism products. The data of each user is than uploaded to a database and aggregated for further processing with a specific analysis software.

ServiceFollow

The web-based analysis software ServiceFollow visualises the touchpoint sequences of different users as a touchpoint matrix. While the rows visualise each customer journey as a horizontal sequence of touchpoints, columns can be used to represent the same touchpoints of different users. Hence, if sequences differ between users blank fields occur. Touchpoints can be arranges simply by drag-and-drop – just as if they were digital sticky notes. The users' touchpoint assessments are aggregated to mean values to identify critical incidents immediately. These critical touchpoints (positive or negative) and its consolidated documentations can be the starting point for further in-depth research. Furthermore, not only customers can use mobile ethnography to capture their customer journey, but also staff and other actors within service processes can use it to document their service journey. Hence, interactions between different stakeholders become evident. Additionally, various customer journeys can be combined on a geographic map whereby clusters of positive or negative touchpoints appear. These clusters and the underlying touchpoints with their detailed documentation are a powerful tool to understand experiences in a destination management context.

This approach contrasts other quantitative but also classic qualitative research approaches through its open approach, which intentionally does not predetermine any certain questions or categories. The guests decide what is a touchpoint during their individual customer journeys and it is them who evaluate and document those by adding text messages, photos, videos or audio files besides meta data such as date, time and GPS position.

How to set up a project with myServiceFellow and ServiceFollow

—— **Project preparation:**
— Agree on research objective.
— Provide incentive for participants.
— Define deadline of field phase.

—— **Pre-field phase (ServiceFollow):**
— Create project and add all basic data.
— Transform research objective into clear instructions
  for the participants.
— Create users.
— Add users to project.
— Test everything.
— Distribute login info to users.
— Be prepared to give support during entire field phase.

—— **Field phase (myServiceFellow):**
— Users log in with their username and password
  (internet connection needed).
— User can add touchpoints and document their service experience with
  text, photos, videos and audio files (no internet connection needed).
— Users upload their data (internet connection needed).

—— **Analysis phase (ServiceFollow):**
— Check if all users uploaded their data.
— Conduct interviews using the customer journey view (optional).
— Arrange touchpoints using the touchpoint matrix (optional).
— Tag touchpoints using the touchpoint matrix (optional).
— Analyse data using the touchpoint matrix, customer journey
  view or map view.

www.myServiceFellow.com

MYSERVICEFELLOW

myServiceFellow is a mobile ethnography application for mobile devices (Apple and Android). Users can download the app for free and log in with a provided username and password. With the app they can document their individual customer journey. They can add touchpoints, evaluate these and document them using text, photo, video and audio files. Besides, date, time and GPS position is tracked.

1 Add a touchpoint
2 Add a photo

SERVICEFOLLOW

ServiceFollow is the web-based analysis software for data gathered with the myServiceFellow app. It is optimised for iPads, but also works on several browsers. A fast internet connection is required when analysing projects.

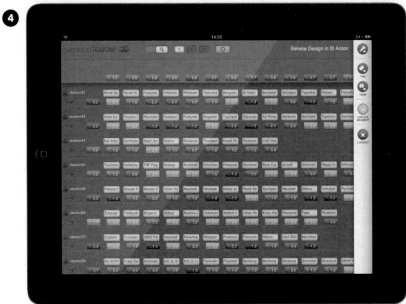

3 The touchpoint matrix (zoomed in)

4 The touchpoint matrix (zoomed out)

5 The customer journey view

6 The map view

5

6

The cases:

CASES

—Jan Huizing, Karoline Wiegerink, Rafaela Rotermund

The general research aim behind the following seven pilot studies is to assess the applicability of myServiceFellow to gain insights about how guests experience services within certain tourism destinations. Using myServiceFellow each case strives to identify relevant touchpoints within the customer journey including highs and lows.

Due to the fact that each case had a different objective, results represent a great diversity. Although the cases reflect only certain aspects of each pilot study, their variety exemplify the broad field where myServiceFellow could be applied.

CHAPTER 5.1

WINTER SPORTS DESTINATION ST. ANTON/AUSTRIA

— *Marc Stickdorn, Birgit Frischhut, Josef Schmid*

FACTS AND FIGURES

WHERE	WHEN	DURATION
Winter sports destination St. Anton am Arlberg, Austria	Dec 29, 2011 – Feb 29, 2012	2 months

WHAT

Guests of St. Anton were encouraged to evaluate service experiences as holiday testers, building on similar-named TV shows that report the daily life of mystery guests in hotels. Comments before, during and after the guest's stay were taken into consideration for the analysis.

GUESTS

Any guest who visited St. Anton during the project could particpate. A general interest to share their experiences was required. Most of them particpated to help the destination to improve further.

42 participants

HOSTS/STAKEHOLDERS

– The tourist board aims to interact with guests to further improve offers as well as enhancing the destination's image.

– Holiday testers use myServiceFellow as a feedback tool, to share with hosts what they like and what they dislike about a service.

– St. Anton's service providers like to know what guests think about their performances and their ideas for improvements.

A CLOSER LOOK INTO THE GUEST EXPERIENCE JOURNEY

How did you hear about St. Anton?

"I saw this picture in a magazine … and then I had only one desire – I want to learn skiing!"

INQUIRING INFORMATION
– Website
– Social media sites
– Blogs
– Tourist Board

Individual bookings
– Hotel website
– Airline
– Train

What did you experience there?

"First time on skies in my life. Yeah, yeah, yeah!"

ACTIVITIES
– Skishow and events
– Après ski and nightlife
– Tobogganing
– Wellness

Necessities to start skiing
– Organizing ski instructor
– Renting ski equipment
– Buying ski wear

What's left from your adventure?

"It's been so much fun! So I'll keep it up until I can do much more advanced skiing".

THAT'S LEFT
– Lots of new friends
– 1001 memories
– 8 GB of pictures and videos
– Ski club membership
– Follower on Twitter
– Fan on Facebook

… and a returning visitor next winter season

INSPIRING EXAMPLES

Highs

*"I went into a sport shop and surprisingly the sales clerk
remembered me from the year before. That was unbelievable".*
"Award-winning steak. Great atmosphere".

Guests were delighted the most when they had an unexpected pleasant experience. This related mostly to very simple things, such as a sales person remembering a former customer or a small welcome present from the landlord. But also restaurants, by far the most often evaluated service, were sometimes able to overwhelm their guests not only with taste, but also with sophisticated food presentations and genuine hospitality.

Lows

"Some things got stolen".
"Someboday tried to steal my skies".

These comments show how quickly a positive experience can turn into a very negative experience once guests discover that their skis disappeared. It is then irrelevant whether they were taken by mistake or purposely stolen.

Such an inconvenience is a general problem that occurs among many Aprés-Ski huts. Although venue operators are not responsible for losses or damages, it leaves a bad impression. But what to do when up to 2000 guests place their skis around one single hut every day?

This is a crucial question that will need to be discussed to avoid such negative experiences.

PILOT PROJECT LEARNINGS

1. from the guest perspective

MyServiceFellow is a powerful tool that enables guests to become actively involved in the development process of St. Anton and its service providers. There is also a demand to share experiences with friends via social media. This missing function would have been appreciated by many of the technique enthusiastic participants.

2. from the host perspective

For service providers it will be increasingly difficult to "get away" with bad services. Therefore criticism should be acknowledged and taken into account for further improvements.

For a detailed analysis of a whole season, it is advised to offer service providers professional consultancy to develop accurate future strategies.

OVERALL IMPRESSIONS

1 Touchpoint (rated: +2 - very positive): "Stunning views"

2 Touchpoint (rated: +1 - positive): "Recycling everywhere. Great!"

3 Touchpoint (rated: -1 - negative): "No public wireless. I would love to post this photo on facebook now!"

4 Touchpoint (rated: +2 - very positive): "Food is really good. The kaisersmarren are fabulous. The interior look really fantastic. The personal is very friendly."

5 ServiceFollow: A customer journey of a guest in St. Anton (anonymised).

6 ServiceFollow: A touchpoint map of St. Anton (anonymised).

5

6

CHAPTER 5.2

GAMLA LINKÖPING CHRISTMAS MARKET IN EARLY 19TH CENTURY ENVIRONMENT IN LINKÖPING/SWEDEN

— Fabian Segelström, Stefan Holmid

FACTS AND FIGURES

WHERE	WHEN	DURATION
Open air museum "Gamla Linköping" (Old Linköping) Linköping, Sweden	Nov 26–27, 2011	2 market days; market open 10am – 4pm on both days

WHAT

Annual Christmas market in neighbourhood constructed of houses moved from other parts of Linköping as the city was modernised from the 1950's and onwards. The neighbourhood also serves as an open air museum, and the market is being hosted by the local Lions chapter.

GUESTS

The event is popular among most segments of society, but with an over-representation of ethnic Swedes. Participants where either pre-recruited or approached and asked about partici-pating at the market.

26 participants

The Christmas market had roughly 17000 visitors during the weekend

HOSTS/STAKEHOLDERS

– The collaboration partner for the study was the open air museum, which wants to understand what attracts visits to Gamla Linköping in general and their markets specifically.

– Lions as organisers of the specific event, and all the exhibitors at the market.

A CLOSER LOOK INTO THE GUEST EXPERIENCE JOURNEY

The app's functionality to attach the GPS location of where the guests are when a touchpoint is added provided us with valuable information in which parts of the market events happened which were deemed as important by the guests themselves. We saw that guests had added large amounts of touchpoints whilst at the square. A probable explanation for this focus on the square is that the square was the scene for a number of performances throughout the weekend. This emphasis on the performances provides interesting insights for the content of coming markets.

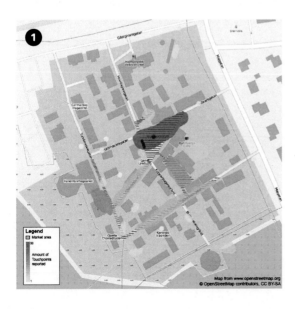

1 Touchpoint Heat Map - This map shows the market area and the amount of added touchpoints.

INSPIRING EXAMPLES

Highs

Crowning of the Lucia of Linköping is an old Swedish tradition, and Lucias are crowned all over Sweden in November and December. The crowning of Linköping happened at the Christmas fair and as a tradition, Lucia and her helpers sang a series of Christmas carols at the coronation. The event was rated +1.64 on average (with +2 being the maximum). Examples of quotes from participants:

"Christmas starts now!"
"Lucia and nice singing – much appreciated"

LOWS

The exhibitors all run small stands where they sell their products, but no one is able to accept credit cards. As many people do not carry cash this lead to problems for many visitors who were not able to shop as they wanted to (leading in turn to a decrease in sales for vendors). The lack of an ATM had an average rating of -1,67 (-2 was lowest possible). As seen in the participant quotes, the fact that there is an old bank building which does not offer bank services adds to the confusion:

"The bank office didn't have an ATM"
"It's odd that there isn't an ATM around, since all vendors only accept cash"

PILOT PROJECT LEARNINGS

1. from the guest perspective

Most guests liked the basic idea behind myServiceFellow, and had suggestions in which directions it could be developed to further improve the value provided by the app.

That being said, many guests (especially those visiting the market with children) raised the issue that using the app felt like it was intruding on their experience of the market visit. Being new to the app and not exactly sure how it works and then using it under a short time frame (most guests were at the market for 1-1,5h) was perceived as stressful. It might be that myServiceFellow and similar tools are better suited for usage over a longer time period than in this case.

2. from the host perspective

The data helped the hosts in reaffirming some things they were already aware of, but also provided them with challenges to solve for future markets. As the host partner was the open air museum (rather than the local Lions organisation), insights provided will help in improving the experience of the open air museum in general.

OVERALL IMPRESSIONS

2 Touchpoint (rated: +1 - positive): "Wonderful environment and atmosphere".

3 Touchpoint (rated: +2 - very positive): "Market".

4 Touchpoint (rated: +2 - very positive): "Lucia and singing:) very fun!"

5 ServiceFollow: The touchpoint map of the Christmas market.

6 ServiceFollow: ServiceFollow: A touchpoint reported during the Christmas market.: "Full trash bin" (rated: -1 - negative).

5

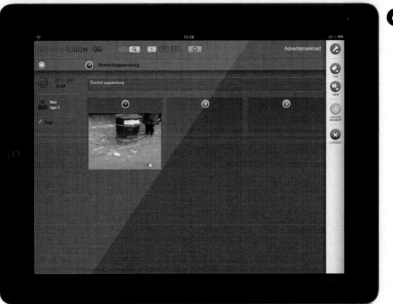

6

CHAPTER 5.3
WINTER SEASON IN HOLIDAY RESORT TAHKO/FINLAND

— *Tiina Kuosmanen*

FACTS AND FIGURES

WHERE	WHEN	DURATION
Holiday resort Tahko, Nilsiä, Central Finland (the Lakeland area)	Dec 27, 2011-Mar 11, 2012	2 months and 12 days

WHAT

Guests who were coming to Tahko area were invited to participate in this project and take part in developing Tahko services through internet, social media, e-mail, posters and personal contacts. At the end of the holiday, all participants were interviewed to get even more detailed information on the touchpoints reported as well as how participants experienced the use of myServiceFellow.

GUESTS

Volunteers, who came to the holiday resort Tahko and spent their holiday with activities, events or enjoying the nature, were able to take part in this project. Volunteers gave feedback about their experiences and feelings before and during their holiday through the app and in an interview at the end of the holiday.

Participants: 33 guests (18 male, 15 female) mostly from Southern Finland

Age: 19-58 years

Duration of stay: 2-4 days

Total touchpoints: 444

HOSTS/STAKEHOLDERS

Tahko area's stakeholders want to know how their guests feel about their services now and how they could develop better services.

Tahko Marketing Company wants to gain new information about Tahko's customers, customer journeys, and what are the main reasons to come to Tahko. Information will be utilized for marketing purposes.

Tourism development companies are interested in how myServiceFellow works in tourism business.

Before holiday

INFORMATION ABOUT TAHKO

– Internet, social media

– Brochure, newspaper

RESERVATION

– By internet

– By phone

TRAVEL TO TAHKO

– By car

– By bus

Expectations

"Every year, this time we make skiing plans with friens." (+2)

"It is easy to make reservations by internet." (+2)

"Great, we got slope, weather and event information to our phone." (+2)

"There were many busses leaving to Tahko."

"We were in front of the booking office, but the bus driver didn't inform why we stopped." (0)

During the holiday

– Arrive to Tahko

– Cottage, hotel

– Restaurant

– Ski and other activities

– Eat

– Ski bus

– Shop

Experiences

"Cottage was perfect, better than in pictures." (+2)

"There were enough snow on the slopes. Fire and wood were ready." (+2)

End of holiday

– Back to home, work, school

– Share experience with friends and family (facebook, face-to-face, etc.)

Image

"Nice weekend, next year again" (+2)

INSPIRING EXAMPLES

Highs

Many participants commented on ski tracks, slopes and nature, restaurant or accommodation. They said skiing areas were in good condition, there were not too many tourists (no queuing) and the view from top of Tahko was beautiful.

Food and service in restaurants were rated good. Customer servants were rated friendly and genuine.

"Thank you, slopes were well maintained" (+2)
"Good, slopes were open every day until 7 p.m." (+2)
"There should be a skiing arena in the future (summer)" (+1)
"Good service and adaptable people." (+1)

Lows

Infrastructure and facilities of holiday homes were commented quite often. Customers expect the holiday homes to have same facilities as they have at home.

"There was no electric kettle". (0)
"There were not many vegetable foods in restaurant." (-1)
"There should be more signposts on the walkway" (-1)

PILOT PROJECT LEARNINGS

1. from the guest perspective

Participants regard myServiceFellow as easy and comfortable to use as they can intuitively give feedback and take part in the development process.

„Best was to give feedback in real time."

The app would be better if it could be also used by Windows-based devices and if there was a possibility to communicate through social media. Using the application emptied the battery quickly and the cold weather affected the functionality of the device.

2. from the host perspective

The hosts like this application because it is versatile and easy to use, it gives reports of customer journeys and helps detecting problems in services quickly.

Many basic customer surveys and customer feedback apps provide customer insights before and after the vacation. The app provides detailed information and experiences from the customers during the vacation. Tahko area customer surveys usually have been made by individual companies from their point of view but the app enables to study customer journeys from the point of view of the whole holiday resort.

OVERALL IMPRESSIONS

1 Touchpoint (rated: +2 – very positive): "Beautiful landscape".

2 Touchpoint (rated: +1 – positive): "There are enough lean-tos and in the right place".

3 Touchpoint (rated: +2 – very positive): "We were skiing and we saw reindeers!"

4 Touchpoint (raited:+2 – very positive): "Slopes were good condition and open until 7 p.m".

5 ServiceFollow: Customer journey of a guest in Tahko (anonymised).

6 ServiceFollow: A touchpoint map of several guests in Tahko (anonymised).

5

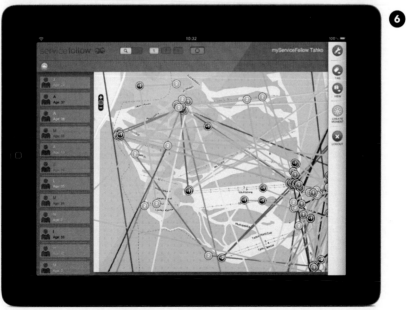

6

CHAPTER 5.4

A TOUR OF THE TOWN ANTIBES JUAN LES PINS AND MOUGINS/FRANCE

— *Girish Prayag, Frédéric Dimanche, Mady Keup*

FACTS AND FIGURES

WHERE	WHEN	DURATION
Antibes Juan les Pins and Mougins, French Riviera	Winter 2012	2 independent pilots each lasting 1 half day

WHAT

The project was related to city and village visitors touring a destination. myServiceFellow was tested at two French Riviera destinations with the help of local tourism offices: Antibes Juan Les Pins and Mougins. The tests took place on separate winter half days during the low season.

GUESTS

Visitors to Antibes and Mougins

Antibes: 17 participants

Mougins: 38 participants

Guests were recruited among SKEMA international students who had never visited the destinations.

HOSTS/STAKEHOLDERS

– Antibes Office of Tourism, its director, communication team, and tour guides. They want to see how the old town is perceived.

– Mougins Office of Tourism, whose director recently installed QR code stations at various points in the village. They want to test how tourists use the itineraries and the QR stations.

A CLOSER LOOK INTO THE GUEST EXPERIENCE JOURNEY

The project was conducted at two destinations on the French Riviera: First, Antibes Juan Les Pins, a coastal destination with a medieval urban core. In this setting, visitors were recruited to test the application in the context of a tour of the old town. Second, Mougins, a hill village known for its galleries, culinary arts, and for having been one of Picasso's residences while living on the French Riviera recently established and wanted to test QR code stations posted throughout the village.

Visitors are greeted and briefed at the tourist office; once equipped with their mobile device and the app, they are going on a tour of the destination.

In Antibes, they are accompanied by a guide through the streets of the old town; as they follow the guide, they identify touchpoints that affect their touring experience and indicate their perceptions of the various aspects of the itinerary. Some are attractions; some are urban occurrences that tourism professionals may not pay attention to.

In Mougins, they are left to wander as they please in the old village. They do a self-guided tour, exploring the street, and sometimes follow the stop points of interest that are suggested by the Office of Tourism through small posts with a sign. Those 17 signs contain only a sentence of two, but they each have QR codes that allow the connected traveller to find more content about the attraction. Since there is not a logical service flow for the visit (visitors could tour the village as they wish), we propose to highlight some of the results in tabular format, for each of the stop points/QR flash points. Comments were made by visitors during the visit as well as in post-experience interviews.

FLASHPOINTS	VISIBILITY	LEVEL OF INTEREST	STRONG POINTS	WEAK POINTS	RECOMMENDATIONS
Vaste Horizon	YES	4/5	Interesting content (historic aspects)	Too long story	Making shorter
La place Roger Vergé La sculpture de Fani Rigobalti	YES	4/5	Interesting and relevant content	– Repetition of the date 2006 – Very bad and dangerous location (at a crossroad), cars are just allowed until 11:00 am, but families with children are used to visit in the morning	– Do not deal with the inauguration, it lacks interest – We advise putting the flashpoint next to the map (see picture n°…)
La place Lieutenant Isnard	NO	2/5	Short and detailed content	Intricate vocabulary (especially for children)	Explaining the origin of the name "Isnard"
La maison et l'atelier Maurice Gottlob	NO	3/5	Interesting content and well emphasized (spot light: Maurice Gottlob, a famous painter, sculptor and poet)	– Access difficulty: the QR code is not easy to find out – The surrounding is not clean	Adding place signature to show visitors the way
Le centre administratif			Due to the long distance, we didn't visit		
Place du Commandant Lamy – Jardin Gottlob	YES	3/5	In the center of the Village, next to the museum, easy to be a gathering point	– No shops around: as here is the general gathering point, it's possible to add some souvenir shops for visitors – The map of village has no compass and it's difficult to find out the direction	Adding more decoration for the garden
La Mairie – L'Espace Culturel	YES	4.5/5	– Interesting content – Significative place: full of artistic pictures in the hall, multifunction for reception	It may interest, resembling as ancient church (but a marriage hall today)	Establishing some facilities for meeting and attract some artist to launch their works here
L'église Saint-Jacques-le-Majeur	YES	3/5	– Long and interesting historic content – Plenty of meaningful pictures	– The QR code is far away from the church and too difficult to find it – Different information: the opening time from the notice of its door is not the same as real	– Changing the place of QR code (suggestion to put it in the center of two streets as they are over crossing and the board is in inner direction) – Being precise about the opening time

FLASHPOINTS	VISIBILITY	LEVEL OF INTEREST	STRONG POINTS	WEAK POINTS	RECOMMENDATIONS
La rue des Or-fèvres et la rue des Lombards	YES	3/5	– Well located (deep inside the village), with plenty of unique and classi-cal art and antique boutiques – Beautiful street showcasing and enchanting unique art and antique history of village – The decoration of the street still re-spects the ancient style, with an air of antiquity	The street is not enough highlighted with flowers for example	Different kinds of flowers with different florescence should be planted to make the place beautiful in all seasons
La place Albicocco	NO	3/5	Relevant information about a famous pho-tographer who died in Mougins	– Lack of introduc-tion of this famous people and pho-tos in this place – The place is not quite special	Adding some introduc-tion and photos, it could describe the precise place and reason of death for this famous people
La porte Sarrazine	YES	5/5	Interesting con-tent / augmented re-ality (very concrete, we believe it)		
Le four à pain	YES	2/5	Cultural aspect of the content (bread related to France and bread oven very important for a village)	The place doesn't seem realistic, it's very difficult to im-agine a bread oven there (not interesting for everybody)	
Place des Mûriers et la Maison du Com-mandant Lamy	YES	5/5	Interesting content (with examples and a story)	A lot of information which are not visible directly from the flashpoint location	– Giving more time to people to move from a place to another – Creating a button where to click to access the second (rue du Moulin) and third (impasse) information
La Renaudière	YES	2/5	Knowing that this is the house of J. Brel	– The story of the pilot is not interesting – It's easy to miss it because of the narrow alley – No introduction and pictures about this person	– We expect more to know briefly who was J. Brel (especially for for-eigners) and almost his story related the village – Make QR code easier to see
Le Relais de la Poste	YES	3/5	Rue Honoré Henry (ancient mayor of Mougins)	No picture to reveal him	Adding his photo or video to talk about his generosity and work to the village
Le Lavoir	YES	3/5	An unique place for temporary exposition	No obviously sign to point out that's an exhibition hall	Adding some sign for the exhibition
La place des Patriotes	YES	5/5	Interesting to locate other villages	Problem for the flash point if somebody is seat on the bench	Creating an interactive map with other villages to augment reality

INSPIRING EXAMPLES

Highs

A visitor is flashing a QR code at the entrance of the village. She found the QR codes very useful and easy to use. Comment from a participant:

"Mougins is one of the most beautiful villages. It's great to wander through the small streets and to discover little gems at each corner."

LOWS

Comment from participants:

"The old picturesque village creates a wonderful historical experience by itself and I think that the interference with high technology partly ruins this moment because I was more focused on finding the signs than having a pleasant visit. I don't think that this kind of e-visit is useful enough for an old village; the visit by our own provides enough experience in our point of view."
"Too bad the content is only in French!"

PILOT PROJECT LEARNINGS

1a. from the guest perspective, positive
"Very easy to use".
"Some of the tools in the applications are like the camera we already use on a daily basis".
"You can use it offline".
"It has geolocalisation potential".

1b. from the guest perspective, negative

——— Participants had problems with the video function.

——— They do not like the use of smileys before taking pictures.

——— Not being able to add more pictures to the same touchpoint.

——— With android, the function of picture and video did not work.

——— Once the data is uploaded, you cannot get back to the pictures, you might want to keep the pictures.

——— Not possible to delete some of the touchpoints.

2a. from the hosts' perspective, Antibes
"An excellent opportunity to identify and track reasons for dissatisfaction".
"Tourists pay attention to things we did not consider important;
this will help improve our tour guiding".
"The tool gives visitors an opportunity to "see" things we otherwise
would not pay attention to".
"It is a great tool that complements our quality management strategy."

2a. from the hosts' perspective, Mougins
"Although QR codes may detract from the visitor experience, they prove to be useful".
"We have identified weak points that we need to improve on before the
beginning of the season".

OVERALL IMPRESSIONS

1 Touchpoint (rated: +2 - very positive): "Best welcoming city ever".

2 Touchpoint (rated: +1 - positive): "QR Code".

3 Touchpoint (rated: +2 - very positive): "Streets where artists used to live".

4 Touchpoint (rated: +1 - positive): "Gorgeous city hall. Nice building with lovely art indoor".

5 ServiceFollow: Customer journey of a guest in Mougins.

6 ServiceFollow: A touchpoint map of a guest in Mougins.

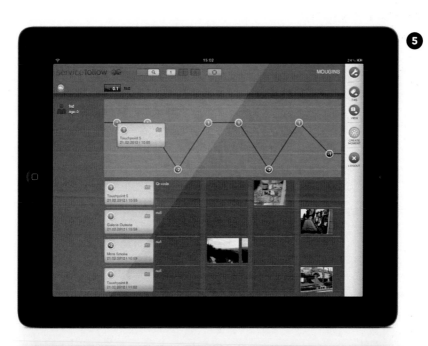

5

6

CHAPTER 5.5

THE "PARENT'S DAY" JOURNEY HOTELSCHOOL THE HAGUE/NETHERLANDS

— *Jan Huizing, Karoline Wiegerink, Rafaela Rotermund, Danilo Huss*

FACTS AND FIGURES

WHERE	WHEN	DURATION
Hotelschool The Hague, The Hague, Netherlands	Oct 29, 2011 Jan, 28 2012	Each journey lasted around one day – depending on the travel distance to and from The Hague

WHAT

Parents who confirmed their attendance at the school's "Parent's Day" were invited to take part in the project. They were asked to use myServiceFellow to document how they experience their dive into their children's study life.

GUESTS	HOSTS/STAKEHOLDERS
Parents who followed the invitation of their children to participate at "Parent's Day" in order to experience their study and work life in the Hague 26 participants	– The Hotelschool aims to build up good relationships between the institution and the students as well as their parents with demonstrating the work environment and study content. – The students who want to show their work and progress to their parents and relatives. – The municipality gains response on the means of travel and their convenience to get there.

A CLOSER LOOK INTO THE GUEST EXPERIENCE JOURNEY

Parents were contacted with the needed information and log in details of myService-Fellow in advance to their arrival. Therefore the journey started with the arrival continued with fixed touchpoints in school and ended with their departure experience.

THE "PARENTS DAY" JOURNEY

Preparation	Arrival	Hotelschool	Departure	Post visit
Receiving the "parents day" invitation	Driving to The Hague by car	Being welcomed by a "flashmob" of enthusiastic and motivated children	Sadly saying goodbye to our children	Filling out feedback questionnaire
Receiving project information	Stopping at gas station	Listening to welcome speech and project introduction	Leaving the Hotelschool	Sharing experience with our children, family and friends
Receiving myServiceFellow log-in details	Arriving in The Hague	Happy to see how my daughter looked beautiful in her uniform	Paying really high parking fee	
	Trying to find Hotelschool and parking possibility		Leaving The Hague	
	Arriving at the Hotelschool The Hague		Standing in traffic jam	
			Annoying speed limit for no reason	

INSPIRING EXAMPLES

Highs

"Heart shaped Welcome"

The most inspiring example, the heart shaped welcome, reflects that simple and small things catch the customers' attention and make it memorable. Symbols seem to lead the steps of a journey.

Lows

"Workshops were interesting but too many, it was even a bit exhausting"

Even though the parents enjoyed the journey with interesting workshops, it lasted a negative impression. This feedback helps to find a better balance in setting up the journey in order to retain a positive impression for future journeys.

PILOT PROJECT LEARNINGS

1. From the guest perspective

"When I am taking a journey, I want to enjoy it instead of keeping track of everything".

——— Shows that even with a mobile and handy device like myServiceFellow, a feedback on the experiences of the journey is not guaranteed.

"Based on new concept and better than using questionnaires".

——— Shows that people want to give feedback in a more "state of the art" and innovative way.

"Anonymous and individually decision what to mention".

——— People still want to be anonymous when giving feedback.

——— People want to have the choice when and about what they express their perception.

"Great mobility, easy to operate and many options to express impressions".

——— Mobility and accessibility seems to play an important role in today's society.

——— People want to spread their experience fast and quick by picture, video or voice record.

"Formulating longer texts were not possible/only possible to upload 5 touchpoints".

——— People do not want any limitations.

2. From the host perspective

From the hosts perspective the Parents Day Journey offers a great opportunity to make their parents proud of their work and studies. The other point of view and perception by the parents help in the time planning and structuring of any future event. Due to the immediate and anonymous feedback opportunity, the hosts receive information on things that might matter for parents but have not been discovered as a touchpoint by the host.

From the municipal perspective the guest perception can help in topics like parking situation, traffic control and attractiveness of tourist destination based on design and infrastructure.

Overall the stakeholders profit from the guests perceptions which have been immediately submitted to consider any improvements.

OVERALL IMPRESSIONS

1 The dinner during parents day.

2 Students serve a multi-course menu.

3 Students prepare the food for the parents day dinner.

4 Touchpoint (rated: +2 – very positive): "Started in Zinq, then the kitchen followed by Le Debut. Good presentations by our hosts. We saw all the good facilities in the school and ended with a big applause the tour".

5 ServiceFollow: Customer journey of a mother at parents day (anonymised).

6 ServiceFollow: A touchpoint during the parents day documented with several photos (anonymised).

5

6

CHAPTER 5.6

SUMMER DESTINATION JUIST, AN ISLAND IN THE NORTH SEA/ GERMANY

—— *Daniel Amersdorffer, Daniel Sukowski*

FACTS AND FIGURES

WHERE	WHEN	DURATION
Summer destination Juist, an island in the German North Sea region and quite remotely situated (access only by ferry or plane)	August 2011	1 month

WHAT

Within the destination, holiday testers were encouraged to evaluate meaningful service experiences. Comments before, during and after the guest's stay where appreciated for the analysis.

GUESTS

Any volunteer owning a smartphone or willing to borrow one from the tourism bureau in Juist and interested to help improving the destination by feedback via myServiceFellow.

Participants: 22 guests

HOSTS/STAKEHOLDERS

– The tourist board aims to interact with guests to further improve offers as well as enhancing the destination's image.

– Holiday testers use myServiceFellow as a feedback tool, to share with hosts what they like and what they dislike about a service.

– Juist's service providers like to know what guests think about their performances and their ideas for improvements.

Making holidays on the island Juist is very special

The island of Juist is a nature destination where car traffic is not allowed and everything has to be transported by horse wagons. The airport is about 4 kilometers away from the village Juist (the main tourism hotspot) and the ferry port is close to the village – but ferries are just accessing the island once a day due to tides. Visitors to Juist are mostly people above 45 years and not primarily new media enthusiasts. The island's people are rather traditional and the tourism is organized in the way it has been the last decades as a health resort at the seaside – innovation in tourism is a rare phenomenon here and mostly driven by the marketing department of the local tourism authorities (so called Kurverwaltung) or single tourism providers with given tourism knowhow (e.g. 4 star hotels). The innovation unfriendly climate may result from the remote location, the inhabitants mental attitude towards "new things from outside the island" and the missing economical pressure, which results from a stable tourism development lasting for decades.

From the guest's perspective the customer journey is divided into the 5 stages of travelling (dreaming, planning, booking, experiencing, sharing), of which the following two phases were part of the pilot project's perspective:

——— Information and booking – those guests who installed the app myServiceFellow before starting their journey were kindly asked to evaluate their experiences in the information and booking stage.

——— The experience of travelling – especially the journey to Juist was worth its own perspective, because it is quite complex compared to other Islands (ferry once a day, luggage cannot be transported by car on the island, etc.) – but also during their stay guests extensively used myServiceFellow.

INSPIRING EXAMPLES

Highs

"Swimming course for our small children: every year a perfect experience! Friendly trainer, competent staff and a lot of fun for our dear children!"

„Fresh fish, either well prepared in the restaurant's kitchen or for taking it home to your own kitchen. During opening hours, there are often many people and you have to wait quite a time. But it is worth to wait."

Guests were often delighted about very simple things. The positive comments regarding touchpoints rated +1 or +2 never mentioned single things but rather a situation or an evaluation of a whole tourism provider – e.g. a fish restaurant. The media uploaded wasn't helpful at all, because people took e.g. a photo of a restaurant as the whole building, instead of the good fish dish or the people waiting for their fishes to take them home.

Lows

"Very good service, nice ambience, but unfortunately the smell of the dish cleaner destroyed our good experience ..."

"Furthermore an electric fence directly besides to a children's playground is a rather stupid idea."

"Roof at the ticketing counter of the ferry place is too small. When there are more people waiting and when it is raining you are totally wet and frozen after buying tickets."

The negative comments were quite different from the positive ones – because they most often mentioned a special problem and not a complex situation or a whole tourism provider's place. This is kind of useful, because very detailed knowledge about service problems is created – now it is easy to improve those pain points because hints from the guests are really detailed.

Especially things from the journey to the destination normally cannot be remembered in a classic survey during the stay – the app conserves such remembrances.

PILOT PROJECT LEARNINGS

1. from the guest perspective

The guests of Juist are a rather older target group and not very familiar with smart-phones and digital media. Consequently the app should have provided the easiest usability possible. Some improvements concerning the usability and simplicity would be necessary.

The guests enjoyed the idea of being active holiday testers and having responsibility to improve their favourite destination. Juist has had a lot of returning guests for many seasons. These people can often give noteworthy comments and insights if the project manages to motivate them using the app. Communicating the users as holiday testers was helpful because some famous TV shows (RTL, SAT1) involving the subject of testing holidays created a great acceptance for such projects.

The guests often rated rather complex touchpoints, not single process steps of services offered by tourism providers of Juist. Thus it was sometimes very difficult to correctly interpret the given evaluations. Interviews with each participant by the project manager really helped a lot in understanding some of the touchpoints.

Some guests stated in the interviews after using the app that they would like to experience changes in quality and especially in touchpoints they had rated. If the destination organisation of Juist doesn't succeed in bringing the tourism providers to use the knowledge created by myServiceFellow, then the projects sustainability might be questioned by guests and third parties.

2. from the host perspective

The hosts were happy to gain advantages from a project and tool financed by the European Union. As soon as they had to work and use the results for improving their service, the acceptance of the project rapidly dropped a bit and only tourism providers with a professional tourism education kept interest in the project and tried using the project's results.

The project and the app myServiceFellow both had the aim to explore service quality in tourism offers and infrastructure of Juist. This aim was clearly fulfilled as the data generated by the holiday testers showed. Now the next step would be necessary: Provide help and suitable strategies to kick-off a service design prototyping and implementation process. This is an interesting chance for other research projects to find ways in conducting the second and third service design phases.

OVERALL IMPRESSIONS

1 The main beach of Juist with the typical beach chairs.

2 An incomparable sunset at the North Sea island Juist.

3 Touchpoint (rated: +2 - very positive): "Great signage everywhere on the island".

4 Touchpoint (rated: +2 - very positive): "Going by taxi is always nice".

5 ServiceFollow: A touchpoint map of several guests on Juist (anonymised).

6 ServiceFollow: Customer journey of a guest on Juist on the map (anonymised).

5

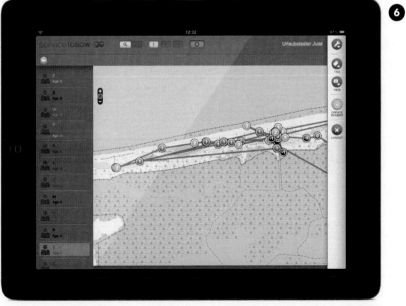

6

CHAPTER 5.7

HURTIGRUTEN CRUISE/ NORWAY

— *Andrea Plesner, Simon Clatworthy*

FACTS AND FIGURES

WHERE	WHEN	DURATION
Hurtigruten cruise boat from Bergen to Kirkenes and back, Norway	Jan 16, 2012 – Jan 19, 2012	4 days

WHAT

Passengers were asked to provide feedback on their journey with Hurtigruten. All participants were interviewed during and after the test, to elaborate on their touchpoints and how they felt using myServiceFellow.

GUESTS

Guests who had booked their cruise were asked by email if they would like to participate. In addition participants were also recruited onboard. All participants received a book and could win a sweater from Dale (both popular items amongst the guests) as compensation.

11 participants, age 47 to 75. Most of the participants were not familiar with smartphones. All participants used iPods that were loaned to them during the test.

HOSTS/STAKEHOLDERS

– Hurtigruten wanted to get a deeper understanding of their customers' needs and how they perceive the quality of the service.

– Tourists on the cruise used myServiceFellow as a feedback tool, to share with Hurtigruten what they like and what they dislike about the service.

A CLOSER LOOK INTO THE GUEST EXPERIENCE JOURNEY

Before the journey
– Get information about the journey
– Book tickets
– Travel to port (plane/bus/train/taxi)

"I came to see the Northern Lights and the cold exotic scenery"

During the stay on board
– Get overview over ship
– Find cabin
– Unpack / get settled
– Find restaurant
– Eat
– Go out on deck to look for Northern Light
– Or stay inside and view through window
– What to do if seasick?
– Get information of ongoing activities
– Join excursions when at different ports
– Be sure to be back to port before boat leaves

"The first day we had some problems finding the way out on the deck."

"The on board information system works very well. Always updated."

"Surprised that is was so little snow to see. Climate change?"

"There is an info button in my cabin announcing if there is Northern Light to be seen during the night. Great!"

"When the ship entcountered the force 8 gale many passengers were ill. The staff acted admirably giving comfort and aid very well."

After the journey
– Travel home (plane/bus/train/taxi)
– Share experience with friends and family
– Keep sounvenirs
– Many guests come again the next year

"The coffee mug will make a great souvenir."

INSPIRING EXAMPLES

Highs

Many passengers commented on the Hurtigruten coffee deal (Buy the cup, get as much coffee from the machines as you like during your whole journey):

"The coffee deal is a really good idea".

"Coffee deal: The mug is effective on that it keeps the contents warm and it will be a good souvenir".

Also, guests appreciated that they could get Northern Lights wakeup calls in their cabin. Many guests go on this journey specifically to see the Northern Lights:

"We really like the fact that we can get the middle of the night intercom announcements in our room".

Lows

There seems to be a mismatch between customer expectations (due to prices) and service experience. In general guests consider Norwegian prices rather high. This is mentioned frequently. The popularity of the coffee deal indicates that the feeling of getting something for free adds value to the experience. This could be explored further to find what small details can contribute to make up for the fact that Norwegian prices are high.

"Although I'm sure that there's not a lot you can do about it, the prices on board are expensive and as such a disincentive to purchase anything."

PILOT PROJECT LEARNINGS

1. from the guest perspective
Most users found myServiceFellow a relevant and fun tool to use. Most of the users were not experienced with smartphones. Still, after a thorough introduction, they managed very well with adding touchpoints.

"I am more honest (also about the negative feedback) with the app than I would be with a normal shallow survey form".

"I would like to keep the touchpoints as memories".

2. from the hosts' perspective
Through the use of the app Hurtigruten got rich insights into the passenger's experience: small details are mentioned that wouldn't necessarily be discovered through a regular customer survey:

"Panorama lounge: This is a lovely lounge. And, while there is plenty of room to sit, the seats facing forward are often "reserved". It would help if at the welcome talk that guests were told to remove their books, coats etc. when they left the lounge rather than reserving the seats until they came back."

The feedback is more detailed than Hurtigruten would get from the regular survey form they use:

"We really like the fact that we can get the middle of the night intercom announcements in our room. We just responded to one announcement that Nordlys were on the port side. We went to the observation lounge on deck 7. Unfortunately, even though the lights in the panorama room were muted, there was still too much inside and deck side light so we could not see the Nordlys. Fortunately we had brought our winter gear with us so we could go outside right away. We found a number of dark areas along the 5th deck walkway and on the 7th floor back deck. We enjoyed the show, which was subtle but thrilling. Of course with the wind chill from the combined ship speed and nature's wind being rather nippy (as in freezing all exposed skin), we were not able to stay outdoors to watch as long as we wanted. So a suggestion is to mount a webcam at one or more good (dark) spots on the ship and have a TV channel that would allow viewing in the warmth of the inside. I do admit we are wimps!"

OVERALL IMPRESSIONS

1 Touchpoint (rated: +1 - positive): "Nice to go for a walk in the city".

2 Touchpoint (rated: 0 - neutral): "Cabin. Looks old".

3 Touchpoint (rated: +2 - very positive): "The cabin had many nice touches such as the coat rack seen in this picture".

4 Touchpoint (rated: +2 - very positive): "Buses for excursion to Nordkapp".

5 ServiceFollow: Customer journey of a guest on Hurtigruten cruise.

6 ServiceFollow: The cabin as a touchpoint of a guest on Hurtigruten cruise (anonymised).

5

6

6

LESSONS LEARNED

— Andrea Plesner, Simon Clatworthy

During 2011 and 2012 *myServiceFellow* has been tested
in various tourism destinations in seven countries.
In order to recruit tourists to participate in the survey
incentives were needed. Therefore users would receive
compensation for participating and/or they could
win a prize like a one week holiday or a beach chair. The
touchpoints uploaded by the users typically contained
photos and text. Some users added video but the voice
recorder function was rarely used.

Guests mentioned that it felt more modern to use
myServiceFellow for user surveys than using regular
forms for rating a service. The users appreciated
the possibility to individually decide what to mention
and evaluate.

CHAPTER 6.1

ADVANTAGES OF MYSERVICEFELLOW

Rich and accurate feedback

By using myServiceFellow, the service providers got rich feedback on how their guests perceived their services. Since the tool "followed" the guest during the whole journey, the feedback was very accurate. Small details were mentioned that would not necessarily be discovered through using a regular customer survey:

"We really like the fact that we can get the middle of the night intercom announcements in our room. We just responded to one announcement that Northern Lights were on the port side. We went to the observation lounge on deck 7. Unfortunately, even though the lights in the panorama room were muted, there was still too much inside and deck side light so we could not see the Nordlys. Fortunately we had brought our winter gear with us so we could go outside right away. We found a number of dark areas along the 5th deck walkway and on the 7th floor back deck. We enjoyed the show, which was subtle but thrilling. Of course with the wind chill from the combined ship speed and nature's wind being rather nippy (as in freezing all exposed skin), we were not able to stay outdoors to watch as long as we wanted. So a suggestion is to mount a webcam at one or more good (dark) spots on the ship and have a TV channel that would allow viewing in the warmth of the inside. I do admit we are wimps!"

Touchpoint uploaded by a guest at Hurtigruten, Norwegian pilot study.

The data was very comprehensive and supported the data that the service providers already had from decades of experience working hands-on with guests. The findings showed that the use of myServiceFellow clearly exposed the weaknesses of the current service systems and can be a great help when prioritizing where to start improving service experiences.

Guests can choose themselves what to rate

Since the guests choose themselves what to rate, the feedback was both interesting and surprising:

"Panorama lounge: This is a lovely lounge. And, while there is plenty of room to sit, the seats facing forward are often "reserved". It would help if at the welcome talk that guests were told to remove their books, coats etc. when they left the lounge rather than reserving the seats until they came back."

Touchpoint uploaded by a guest at Hurtigruten, Norwegian pilot study

Negative touchpoints were often described more accurately than positive ones. For example, a typical positive touchpoint could be "this restaurant is great" combined with a photo of the restaurant. A negative touchpoint could be:

"An electric fence directly besides to a children's playground is a rather stupid idea."

Touchpoint uploaded by a guest on Juist, German pilot study

GPS

An advantage of the tool was the GPS-function. Tourism responsibles can geographically track the customer's journey through the destination. Furthermore hot spots with many positive or negative comments can be evaluated. The function is however limited on ships (case of Hurtigruten) or sometimes in the mountains (case of St. Anton).

CHAPTER 6.2
CHALLENGES

Time consuming

The recruitment process was time consuming, as it required individual emails with user data to be sent to each user. It would be a great improvement if this action could be automatised.

The analysis software ServiceFollow would benefit from improvements to make it easier getting an overview of uploaded data. Text heavy touchpoints are great for detailed feedback, but the software as it is today does not support long touchpoints in the overview. The software should offer a way to cluster data in certain groups. A generator to make a report document would also be helpful.

Quality of feedback

The quality of the touchpoints was very diverse. Some touchpoints only contained a title and a smiley; some were very comprehensive with text and photos. The challenge is to get valuable feedback that is detailed, to the point and written in a way that cannot be misunderstood. How to turn the regular guest into a professional test user?

CHAPTER 6.3
RECOMMENDATIONS

Wi-Fi and equipment

Stable Wi-Fi is not crucial for using myServiceFellow but it makes the interview at the end of the test go smoother, when scrolling through the uploaded touchpoints in ServiceFollow during the interview.

It works better when participants use their own phone and download the app instead of borrowing equipment – they are familiar with the functionality of the device and less time is needed for introduction. It is also cheaper than lending out equipment.

When using the application in cold weather (Tahko, Finland) there was a problem with the batteries discharging quickly. Such issues might affect the number of uploaded touchpoints.

Duration of the user testing

To get a holistic view of the tourists' journey myServiceFellow should be used during the whole journey. The tool works better when used over several days than if it is used on a service that spans only over a few hours. Users do not want to make touchpoints too frequently and the assignment to upload a given number of touchpoints becomes too intense when the field phase is only a few hours. Users expressed that "When I am taking a journey, I want to enjoy it instead of keeping track of everything".

MyServiceFellow should be supported by a personal interview

The personal interview at the end of the analysis was very helpful in understanding how guests experience their touchpoints and contributed to a deeper insight. Some guests did not want to participate when they heard about the interview in the end, so it might be an idea to make this interview optional for the participants (keeping in mind that some insights then might get lost though).

MyServiceFellow is a great tool for collecting raw data from the users. It is suggested however that the service providers use professional consultancies to interpret the data and develop suitable future strategies based upon results.

How to motivate users

To ensure valuable feedback users need to be dedicated and motivated. The recruitment of users should be given special attention and users should get a thorough briefing on what to do and how to give valuable feedback.

Several users requested the possibility to be able to keep touchpoints as memories and be able to share them with friends via social media. This is not possible with the app today but should be explored as an additional functionality and a possible incentive for tourists to use myServiceFellow.

MyServiceFellow is a powerful tool that enables guests to become actively involved in the development process of the destination and its service providers. It gives the user the feeling to have a direct influence on the service. Therefore it is important that once the users have given their feedback that they see that things have changed when they come back the next year. At least those small things that are easy to change.

7

OUTLOOK
TO THE FUTURE

— Daniel Sukowski, Daniel Amersdorffer

Service design represents a new way of thinking – at least in the tourism industry. Service is all about the customer's point of view and service design helps to understand this perspective and to design appropriate service systems. However, to achieve this, service design thinking should be regarded as a holistic management approach and applied throughout the whole organisation.

CHAPTER 7.1

INCREASING IMPORTANCE OF SERVICE DESIGN IN TOURISM – ESPECIALLY IN TIMES OF DIGITAL CONSUMPTION

The internet became the infrastructure of our times. It answers questions and helps us to solve everyday problems such as purchase decisions. In fact, nowadays the internet is such an important part of our society that it would be impossible to handle many daily-life situations without it. This development implicates the need for new business strategies – particularly in the travel and tourism industry, since customers cannot test tourism products in advance.

The internet changes the purchase decision process. Before a purchase the internet provides important information to evaluate a certain product. As published in the AGOF-Study „internet facts 2010-II", this applies particularly to tourism services. The study reveals that this results from the fact that a holiday is not a tangible product which can be tested before a purchase. Therefore, trustworthy sources such as the shared experiences of others guests become more and more important.

Why is service design becoming more and more important?
The transparency of a product through social media and the relevance of user-generated content, such as online reviews, result in a rising demand of customers regarding service quality.

Tourism stakeholders cannot anymore repress those influences with classic advertising. Only high-quality and extraordinary experiences will spread via word-of-mouth through social networks. This process happens without any assistance of tourism service providers and/or destination management organisations.

Three factors define how to gain the customer's attention for a tourism product:

—— **Stories.** Which images create stories about a respective product in the customer's mind?

—— **Authors.** Who are the authors of these stories and are they trustworthy from a customer's perspective?

—— **Channels.** Which channels are involved to reach the customer and do they enjoy public confidence?

From the perspective of a tourism service provider or a destination management organisation, the story about a product is certainly the most important of these three factors, since this is the factor that can be influenced the easiest way. Which channel customers finally choose to tell their stories depends on their own preferences. Only few destinations consider the two latter factors from a strategic and implementation-oriented perspective. Service design offers a great approach to understand these stories and systematically create appropriate tourism products considering the stories these arouse, who tells them whom and through which channels.

CHAPTER 7.2

SUCCESS FACTORS OF SERVICE DESIGN IN TOURISM

There are some factors which make or break service design projects in the travel and tourism industry. The following list of success factors for service design in tourism is without any claim to comprehensiveness; though it might serve as a guideline for first projects.

——— **Put the customer in the centre of all reflections.** Working in a user-centred way is inherent in the service design mindset.

——— **Consider everything as a service** – even if it is just a cup of coffee. A service-dominant mindset is crucial for all stakeholders involved in a service design project. A service should be understood as a sequence of human interactions involving guests, employees, but also digital interfaces and tangible products as well as physical infrastructure. This approach enables to design service systems creating meaningful experiences for customers.

——— **Increase cooperation and mutual understanding of stakeholders.** Participants of a service design process need to share the vision that they work towards a seamless tourism experience for their customers. As this involves different services by various stakeholders, mutual trust is crucial.

——— **Work in multi-disciplinary teams.** The composition of a project group for such a co-creative process is important to achieve valuable outcomes. Work groups should include heterogeneous people based in different knowledge networks – both of theoretical and practical nature.

—— **Be aware of the iterative and co-creative process.** Service design bases on an iterative process consisting of various mostly co-creative sessions. This process follows a sequence of diverging and converging insights and ideas. Moreover, it needs to be flexible enough to integrate new findings throughout the process. Each session in itself needs to be consciously designed regarding dramaturgy, assuring a safe space for participants allowing a truly (co-)creative workspace.

—— **Service design has to be fun.** Participants of service design workshops should use both their emotional and rational half of the brain, but also include physical exercises. A holistic challenge is vital to maximize creativity and empathy.

—— **Do not stop with the concept.** Agree on the outcome of a service design project beforehand and consider how to communicate the results. A project should not stop with a great concept; it needs to include the process of how to implement it in real life. Assure the commitment of all stakeholders involved throughout the implementation process and develop a manageable and endurable change process.

CHAPTER 7.3

IMPLEMENTING SERVICE DESIGN IN TOURISM

It's all about the customer's perception. If service design is used well-conceived, it can be a powerful approach. The results are value propositions meeting customer's needs – even those needs that customers are not yet aware of. Moreover, service design projects can improve employees' working conditions and support the implementation of a sustainable business strategy.

Service design is not a future concept but rather a practiced approach in many industries. Only few companies apply such an user-centred approach in the travel and tourism industry, though. Mostly these are large multi-national organisations, since small and medium-sized enterprises (SMEs) lack the resources to hire external agencies. However, often tourism entrepreneurs of these SMEs already live the basics of service design thinking in their daily life, e.g. when they talk with their guests at the hotel bar for several hours, listening to the problems they had finding a room or when they work with their employees in direct contact with guests observing pointless procedures, or when they handle problems with external stakeholders such as receiving dirty towels from a laundry service. Although there are certainly entrepreneurs who might not need to learn and apply service design for their own business, these are rather the exception. And even for them, service design can be a very valuable approach when they need to work together with other stakeholders within their service ecosystem, e.g. their destination.

How can service design be used to create future tourism products?
Caused by rising importance of positive service experiences and the necessity for a conscious creation and communication of services, service design offers a possibility to make tourism services fit for the future. Service design could be regarded as a holistic perspective across various fields of the tourism sector. Based on a customer-centred perspective, the approach reveals the need for collaboration of different players involved in the development process of tourism products and its service ecosystems. Collaborative learning based on service design thinking will be key in the future.

Contrary to a linear innovation process, service design is an iterative process. Unlike classic management thinking, a design process does not aim to avoid mistakes, but to identify them as soon as possible and to find solutions for these, following the motto "fail early, fail cheap, fail safe". What has been practiced in product design for decades is just starting to be adapted to the service sector: Building service prototypes to iteratively improve services before they are launched on the market. How many prototypes are developed for new cars or mobile phones before they hit the markets? How often are tourism products being prototyped before they are launched? So far, this only happens rarely or at a very late stage in the process, e.g. a soft opening.

To answer the question why service design can be such a successful method for the development of tourism products, it is necessary to look at the human brain and its mental activity – the limbic system. If there is a certain harmony between the areas of thinking, feeling and moving, the behaviour of people who are taking part in a service design workshop is changing positively – and innovation can begin! Due to the fact that service design workshops typically follow a simple structure, participants experience that they already know many things of which they are just not aware of. Simple proceedings can retrieve complex knowledge which is then more specific and available.

How to put service design into practise?

Lego bricks for example can play an important role in a service design workshop, as they help to build perceivable environments. Already at a very early stage this can reveal whether a concept works or not.

One of the most important opportunities for tourism products is storytelling – in particular when considering the strong influence of digital media. Storytelling as a method can be implemented as story building with the help of Lego bricks as a kind of 3D scenario technique. To invent and build something that can be touched is particularly important in tourism. Constructivist learning is only possible when we build something. We know this from our childhood: When building a sandcastle, we knew whether it was going to collapse or not. Besides, such methods often induce a flow feeling – the feeling of getting carried away within an activity. In this way excessive demands can be minimized and boredom avoided during workshops. Furthermore, an atmosphere of harmony can be created where emotions, consciousness and mind are conformal to each other (limbic system). Everything that is build hands-on is easier to understand, stays in the participants' heads and participants identify themselves more with the created concept, because each participant can make an obvious contribution to it. Moreover, these concepts can often be communicated more authentically to customers, management and other stakeholders.

Service design combines mental work with physical creativity, such as 3D scenario techniques or enacting. If participants lose their sense of time during the "game" (i.e. the "flow feeling"), they find the most suitable environment for creativity. Managers, marketing directors etc. become kids again. During such a co-creative process, constructive imagination reveals knowledge and translates it straight into new concepts. A co-creative service design process is a constant iteration of identifying mistakes, improving concepts and a reduction of complex processes to a fun degree. Fun can be one of the main factors leading to success of service design projects, since it keeps the energy level during workshops up and fosters creativity.

CHAPTER 7.4

OUTLOOK: SERVICE DESIGN IN TOURISM

Service design goes far beyond mere product development; it can support human re-sources and organisational development as well as strategic change processes.
However, to do so service design thinking needs to be regarded as a holistic management approach and has to be applied throughout the whole organisation.

Develop customer-centred strategies. One of the biggest challenges for tourism companies is the development of integrated customer-centred strate-gies. Hereby integrated refers to the development of strategies concerning all de-partments and functions from marketing to online and offline distribution, from product development to branding, from human resources to internal processes. To design such holistic strategies, service design thinking offers many new possi-bilities for tourism management.

Develop internal processes. Many tourism organisations, particularly on a destination level, face difficulties within organisational structures – often caused by years of building rigid structures and steep hierarchies or by a missing willing-ness to "rethink" of leading executives. Inefficient process sequences, communi-cation channels and also personnel management can be tackled with service de-sign thinking since all internal processes can be regarded as services and as such iteratively optimised.

Develop a service design based management approach. Not only manage-ment needs to realise the importance of service design – it should be incorporated into a company's culture throughout the whole organisation. Organisations have to leave old paths and adapt to a new way of thinking which allows to co-create value with their customers instead of betraying them through over-promises and under-delivery.

Develop omni-channel structures. Today's society already satisfies many needs with digital services. Looking at the customer journey of a tourist, consist-ing of inspiration, information, booking and travel phase, but also experience sharing after the trip, every phase is already connected to digital products such as websites, apps, smartphones, NFC chips, mobile navigation, to name but a few.

Corporate structures have to adjust to this, enabling a seamless customer experience across all possible channels.

Develop appropriate service design tools and methods. Existing service design tools and methods need to be adapted and further developed with regards to specific industries and changing user behaviours, such as the development of the myServiceFellow app in the field of mobile ethnography.

The research project "Service Design as an Approach to Foster Competitiveness and Sustainability of European Tourism" and the development of the myService-Fellow app can be seen as one part within a process towards the development of a professionalised service design toolset. The experiences of these seven pilot projects exemplify how single service design methods such as mobile ethnography can be used to develop destinations driven by customer experiences. It is hoped that this project functions as a starting point towards a movement in which service design thinking will be integrated in tourism organisations and quality improvement programs. Such programs could include training courses for hotels, destinations and other tourism stakeholders interested in the development of customer-centred services systems.

8

MINI-DICTIONARY/ FURTHER READING/ REFERENCES

Service design has its own set of terms which new-comers need to learn. Thus, this chapter provides a mini-dictionary on service design.

Since this publication deliberatively uses a non-academic style, the following chapter offers further readings besides the references used.

CHAPTER 8.1

SERVICE DESIGN MINI-DICTIONARY

— *Fabian Segelström*

CONCEPT	EXPLANATION
Benchmarking	Surveying the competition, with special attention to what they are good at.
(Service) Blueprint	A visualisation technique borrowed from service management. It aims at mapping out all the components needed to successfully deliver the service.
Co-creation	The involvement of various stakeholders in creating service improvements. Co-creation is often done in workshops based on insights gathered by the service designers through design research. In the related fields service marketing and service management co-creation is used to describe the joint effort between employees and customers needed for a service to be delivered.
Cultural probes	A design research technique in which participants are provided a kit of tools to self-document their lives, with a special focus on the aspects which are relevant for the service being designed.
Customer journey (map)	A visualisation technique which documents a customer's journey through the service. It focuses strictly on the customer and thus aspects of the service not used by the example customer are not shown.
Design for service	The idea that we cannot design a service, but rather only design to facilitate service provision. Several academics prefer this term over service design. Also see Touchpoint.
Design research	The various efforts made by the service designers to gain insights into how, why and when the service is used. The insights gathered through design research drive the rest of the design process.
Desktop walkthrough	Mini-enactment of the service on a desktop with the help of figurines and drawings. A quick prototyping method.

CONCEPT	EXPLANATION
Iterative design process	As all ideas are tested with stakeholders, the design process is iterative, meaning that ideas are transformed into prototypes which are tested with stakeholders. These insights lead to improved ideas, which are tested and so on.
Persona	Archetypical customer. Should be based on rigorous research, but as it is a strong communication tool it is often done even without the research. Most designers avoid calling these "fake" personas for personas, rather using names like user profiles.
Prototype	A service idea represented in the physical world in such a way that the qualities of the idea can be tested.
Prototyping	Testing prototypes with stakeholders.
Stakeholder	Anyone which has a stake in the service. Usually there are different layers; directly affected like customers and front-line staff, closely affected like back-office staff and so. Please note that some people do not include customers when they say stakeholders and only refer to the various roles in the service delivery organisation.
Touchpoint	A physical point of interaction in the service. Touchpoints are usually the focus of most of the design work as they are the components of the service which can be designed.
User	Customer in design talk.
Visualisation	A representation of (parts of) the service, which serve as a joint point of departure. Design research is mostly summarised in a series of visualisations.

CHAPTER 8.2

FURTHER READING/ REFERENCES

FURTHER READING

This chapter provides a brief introduction to service design literature. The interested reader is presented with suggestions for where to continue his/her search.

Text books

Stickdorn & Schneider (2010): This is Service Design Thinking
This textbook provides a wide overview of what service design is, and the various disciplines it has been inspired by. It also includes an extended section of the various tools and techniques used by service designers.

Miettinen & Koivisto (2009): Designing Services with Innovative Methods
The first service design textbook in English. The chapters are more focused on summarising early research trends than giving an overview in comparison to "This is Service Design Thinking". The main author Satu Miettinen is also leading the work on a new textbook provisionally called "Service Design with Theory", due to be published in late 2012.

Meroni & Sangiorgi (2011): Design for Services
This book is the most academic of the textbooks published so far, and gives an overview of the move to design for service (see mini-dictionary). Various theoretical angles of the move are highlighted, as well as investigations to possible future directions of the discipline.

Research findings

So far, the main venue for academic research papers has been the ServDes Conference. All papers from the conference can be downloaded from www.servdes.org. For research results into specific aspects of service design, the work of a number of PhD students is a good start:

Blomkvist (2011): Conceptualising Prototypes in Service Design
Explores how prototypes are used in service design, comparing what is known about prototyping from other design fields to the specific challenges of service design.

Han (2010): Practices and Principles in Service Design: Stakeholders, Knowledge and Community of Practice
This thesis explores how the role of the service designer changes during the various stages of the design process.

Segelström (2010): Visualisations in Service Design
Investigates the use of visualisations in service design, with a focus on how visualisations are used to communicate insights from design research.

Wetter Edman (2011): Service Design – A Conceptualization of an Emerging Practice
Investigates the theoretical similarities and dissimilarities of service design with the related field of service management/marketing and design management. Recommended for the reader interested in Service Dominant Logic.

REFERENCES

Abras, C., Maloney-Krichmar, D. & Preece, J. (2004). User-Centred Design. In Bainbridge, W. Encyclopedia of Human-Computer Interaction. Tousand Oaks: Sage Publications.

Anderson, J.C., Narus, J.A., & van Rossum, W. (2006). Customer value propositions in business markets. Harvard Business Review, March, 90–99.

Arnould, E.J. & Price, L.L. (1993). River magic: extraordinary experience and the extended service encounter. Journal of Consumer Research, 20(June), 24–45.

Arnould, E.J. & Wallendorf, M. (1994). Market-Oriented Ethnography: Interpretation Building and Marketing Strategy Formulation. Journal of Marketing Research, Vol. XXXI (November 1994), 484–504.

Bendapudi, N., & Bendapudi, V. (2005). Creating the living brand. Harvard Business Review, 83(5), 124–133.

Berry, L. (1995). On Great Service: A Framework for Action. New York: Free Press.

Bieger, T. (2005). Management von Destinationen. München: Oldenbourg.

Bitner, M.J. (1992). Servicescape: the impact of physical surroundings on customers and employees. Journal of Marketing, 56(April), 57–71.

Buchanan, R. (2001). Design Research and the New Learning. In Design Issues, 17(4). MIT Press, Cambridge, MA, 3–23.

Buhalis, D. (2000). Marketing the competitive destination of the future. Tourism Management, 21(1), 97–112.

Buscher, M., & Urry, J. (2009). Mobile methods and the empirical. European Journal of Social Theory, 12(1), 99–116.

Carbone, L.P. (1998). Total customer experience drives value. Management Review, 87(7), 62.

Chase, R. B. (2004). It's time to get to first principles in service design. Managing Service Quality, 14 (2/3), 126–128.

Cohen, E. (1972). Toward a sociology of international tourism. Social Research, 90(1), 164–189.

Cohen, E. *(1979)*. A phenomenology of tourist types. Sociology, 13, 179–201.

Driver, B.L., Brown, P.J., Stankey, G.H., & Gregoire, T.G. *(1987)*. The ROS planning system. Leisure Sciences, 9, 201–212.

Eason, K. *(1987)*. Information Technology and Organisational Change. London: Taylor & Francis.

Elliot, R. & Jankel-Elliot, N. *(2003)*. Using ethnography in strategic consumer research. Qualitative Marketing Research, 6(4), 215–223.

Fache, W. *(2000)*. Methodologies for innovation and improvement of services in tourism. Managing Service Quality, 10(6), 356–366.

Fetterman, D.M. *(1989)*. Ethnography: Step by step. Newbury Park, CA: SAGE.

Findeli, A. & Bousbaki, R. *(2005)*. The Eclipse of the Product in Design Theory. Proceedigns of EAD'05 conference, Bremen.

Fiske, S.T., & Taylor, S.E. *(1991)*. Social Cognition. New York: McGraw-Hill.

Fitzsimmons, J.A. & Fitzsimmons, M.J. *(2000)*. New Service Development: Creating memorable Experiences. Thousand Oaks: SAGE.

Frischhut, B., Stickdorn, M., Zehrer, A. *(2012)*. Mobile Ethnography as a new research tool for customer-driven destination management – A case study of applied service design in St. Anton/Austria. CAUTHE 2012 Book of Proceedings – The new golden age of tourism and hospitality, Book 2. Melbourne: CAUTHE, 160–166.

Goeldner, C., & Ritchie, J.R.B. *(2006)*. Tourism: Principles, Practices, Philosophies. Hoboken, NJ: Wiley.

Goulding, C. *(2005)*. Grounded theory, ethnography and phenomenology: a comparative analysis of three qualitative strategies for marketing research. European Journal of Marketing, 39(3), 294–308.

Graburn, N. *(1989)*. Tourism: The sacred journey. In Smith, V. (Ed.) Hosts and Guests: The Anthropology of Tourism. Philadelphia: University of Pennsylvania, 21–36.

Grove, S. J., Fisk, R. P., & Dorsch, M.J. (1998). Assessing the theatrical components of the service encounter: a cluster analysis examination. The Services Industry Journal, 18(3), 116–134.

Grove, S.J., & Fisk, R.P. (1992). The service experience as theater. Advances in Consumer Research, 19, 455–461.

Gummesson, E. (1990). Service design. Total Quality Management, 2(2), 97–101.

Gustafsson, A. & Johnson, M.D. (2003). Competing in a Service Economy: How to Create a Competitive Advantage through Service Development and Innovation. San Francisco: Jossey–Bass.

Helkkula, A. (2011). Characterizing the concept of service experience. Journal of Service Management, 22(3), 367–389.

Holloway, C., & Taylor, N. (2006). The Business of Tourism, Harlow, England: Pearson Education.

Homburg, C., Hoyer, W.D., & Fassnacht, M. (2002). Service orientation of a retailer's business strategy: dimensions, antecedents, and performance outcomes. Journal of Marketing, 66(4), 86–101.

Hosany, S., & Witham, M. (2010). Dimensions of cruisers' experiences, satisfaction, and intention to recommend. Journal of Travel Research, 49(3), 351–364.

IUBH (2011). Untersuchung der Bedeutung & Glaubwürdigkeit von Bewertungen auf Internetportalen. Bad Honnef: International University of Applied Sciences.

Jansson, A. (2002). Spatial phantasmagoria: The mediatization of tourism experience. European Journal of Communication, 17(4), 429–443.

Kang, M., & Gretzel, U. (2012). Effects of podcast tours on tourist experiences in a national park. Tourism Management, 33, 440–455.

Kozinets, R. V. (2002). The Field Behind the Screen: Using Netnography for Marketing Research in Online Communities. Journal of Marketing Research, 39(1), 61–72.

Larsen, S., & Mossberg, L. (2007). The diversity of tourist experiences. Scandinavian Journal of Hospitality & Tourism, 7(1), 1–6.

Larsson, R., & Bowen, D.E. (1989). Organization and customer: managing design and coordination of services. Academy of Management Review, 14(2), 213–233.

Lash, S., & Urry, J. (1994). Economies of Signs and Space. London: Sage.

Laws, E. (1998). Conceptualizing visitor satisfaction management in heritage settings: an exploratory blueprinting analysis of Leeds Castle, Kent. Tourism Management, 19(6), 545–554.

Lusch, R.F., Vargo, S.L., & O'Brien, M. (2007). Competing through service: Insights from service-dominant logic. Journal of Retailing, 83(1), 5–18.

Manfredo, M.J., Driver, B.L., & Brown, P.J. (1983). A test of concepts inherent in experience based setting management for outdoor recreation areas. Journal of Leisure Research, 15, 263–283.

Mascarenhas, O.A., Kesavan, R., & Bernacchi, M. (2006). Lasting customer loyalty: a total customer experience approach. Journal of Consumer Marketing, 23(7), 397–405.

McAlexander, J.H., Schoulten, J.W., & Koening, H.F. (2002). Building brand community. Journal of Marketing, 66(1), 38–54.

McCabe, S. (2002). The tourist experience and everyday life. In Dann, G.M.S (Ed.), The Tourist as a Metaphor of the Social World. Wallingford: CABI Publishing, 61–75.

Meyer, C., & Schwager, A. (2007). Understanding customer experience. Harvard Business Review, February, 1–12.

Morelli, N. (2009). Service as value co-production: reframing the service design process. Journal of Manufacturing Technology Management, 20(5), 568–590.

Obenour, W., Patterson, M., Pedersen, P., & Pearson, L. (2006). Conceptualization of a meaning based research approach for tourism service experiences. Tourism Management, 27, 34–41.

Oh, H., Fiore, A.M., & Jeong, M. (2007). Measuring experience economy concepts: tourism applications. Journal of Travel Research, 46(2), 119–132.

Oliver, R. L. (1980). A Cognitive Model of the Antecedents and Consequences of Satisfaction Decisions. Journal of Marketing Research, November, 460–469.

Otto, J.E. & Ritchie, J.B.R. (1996). The service experience in tourism. Tourism Management, 17(3), 165–174.

Parasuraman, A., Zeithaml, V.A., & Berry, L.L. (1985). A conceptual model of service quality and its implications for future research. Journal of Marketing, 49(4), 41–50.

Patricio, L., Fisk, R.P., & eCunha, J.F. (2008). Designing the multi–interface service experiences. Journal of Service Research, 10(4), 318–334.

Pearce, D. (1989). Tourist Development. London: Longman Scientific and Technical.

Pine II, J.B., & Gilmore, J.H. (1998). Welcome to the experience economy. Harvard Business Review, 76(4), 97–105.

Pine II, J.B., & Gilmore, J.H. (1999). The Experience Economy: Work is Theatre & Every Business a Stage. Boston, MA: Harvard Business School Press.

Preece, J., Rogers, Y. & Sharp H. (2002). Interaction Design: Beyond Human-Computer Interaction. New York: John Wiley & Sons, Inc.

Prentice, R.C., Witt, S.F., & Hamer, C. (1998). Tourism as experience: The case of heritage parks. Annals of Tourism Research, 25(1), 1–24.

Price, L.L., Arnould, E.J., & Tierney, P. (1995). Going to extremes: managing service encounters and assessing provider performance. Journal of Marketing, 59(2), 83–97.

Pullman, M.E., & Moore, W.L. (1999). Optimal service design: integrating marketing and operation perspectives. International Journal of Service Industry Management, 10(2), 239–261.

Quan, S., & Wang, N. (2004). Towards a structural model of the tourist experience: an illustration from food experiences in tourism. Tourism Management, 25, 297–305.

Russel, R., & Faulkner, B. (2004). Entrepreneurship, Chaos and the Tourism Area Lifecycle. Annals of Tourism Research, 31(3), 556–579.

Schembri, S. (2006). Rationalizing service logic, or understanding services as experience. Marketing Theory, 6(3), 381–392.

Schmitt, B. (1999). Experiential marketing: A new framework for design and communications. Design Management Journal, 10(2), 10–16.

Shaw, C., & Ivens, J. (2002). Building Great Customer Experiences. New York: Palgrave MacMillan.

Shaw, G., Bailey, A., & Williams, A. (2011). Aspects of the service-dominant logic and its implications for tourism management: examples from the hotel industry. Tourism Management, 32, 207–214.

Shostack, G.L. (1982). How to design a service. European Journal of Marketing, 16(1), 49–63.

Shostack, L. (1985). Planning the service encounter. In J.A. Czepiel, M.R. Solomon, & C. Surprenant (Eds.). The Service Encounter, Managing Employee/Customer Interaction in Service Business. Mass: Lexington Books.

Stamboulis, Y., & Skayannis, P. (2003). Innovation strategies and technology for experienced based tourism. Tourism Management, 24, 35–43.

Stickdorn, M., Frischhut, B. & Schmid, J. (2012). Mobile ethnography as a pioneering research approach for customer-centred destination management in European tourism. Travel and Tourism Research Association Annual Conference 2012 Conference Proceedings.

Stickdorn, M. (2012). Tourism and Service Design Thinking. Touchpoint – The Journal of Service Design, 4(1), 58–61.

Stickdorn, M., & Schneider, J. (2012). Service Design als innovativer Ansatz für kundenzentriertes Change Management. Zeitschrift für Organisations-Entwicklung, 2/2012, 38–44.

Stickdorn, M. & Schneider, J. (2010). This is Service Design Thinking. Amsterdam: BIS Publishers.

Stickdorn, M., & Zehrer, A. (2010). Mobile ethnography: How service design aids the tourism industry to cope with the behavioral change of social media. Touchpoint – The Journal of Service Design, 2(1), 82–85.

Stickdorn, M., Grabmueller, A., Zehrer, A., & Siller, H. (2010). Service Design im Tourismus – Die Erfassung der touristischen Kontaktpunktkette durch mobile Ethnographie. 4. Forschungsforum der österreichischen Fachhochschulen. Pinkafeld: FFH, 204–209.

Stickdorn, M., Zehrer, A. (2009). Service Design in Tourism – Customer Experience Driven Destination Management, Proceedings of the First Nordic Conference on Service Design and Service Innovation, online: www.aho.no/servicedesign09.

Stickdorn, M., Schneider, J. (2009). myServiceFellow: gaining genuine customer insights, Proceedings of the First Nordic Conference on Service Design and Service Innovation, online: www.aho.no/servicedesign09.

Strain, E. (2005). Public Places – Private Journeys: Ethnography, Entertainment, and the Tourist Gaze. New Jersey: Rutgers University Press.

Teixeira, J.G., Patricio, L., Nunes, N.J., Nobrega, L., Fisk, R.P., & Constantine, L. (2012). Customer experience modeling: from customer experience to service design. Journal of Service Management, 23(3), 1–20.

Tussyadiah, I.P. & Fesenmaier, D.R. (2009). Mediating tourist experiences: access to places via shared videos. Annals of Tourism Research, 36(1), 24–40.

Uriely, N. (2005). The tourist experience: conceptual developments. Annals of Tourism Research, 32(1), 199–216.

Urry, J. (1990). The Tourist Gaze. London: SAGE.

Vargo, S.L., & Lusch, R.F. (2004). Evolving to a new dominant logic for marketing. Journal of Marketing, 68(Jan), 1–17.

Vitterso, J., Vorkinn, M., Vistad, O.I., & Vaagland, J. (2000). Tourist experiences and attractions. Annals of Tourism Research, 27(2), 432–450.

Wolcott, H. (1995). Making a Study "More Ethnographic" in Van Maanen, J. (ed.) Representation in Ethnography. London: SAGE.

Ylirisku, S. & Vaajakallio, K. (2007). Situated Make Tools for envisioning ICTs with ageing workers. Proceedings of Include 2007 conference. Helen Hamlyn Research Centre, RCA, UK.

Zehrer, A. (2009). Service experience and service design: concepts and application in tourism SMEs. Managing Service Quality, 19(3), 332–349.

Zeithaml, V.A., Parasuraman, A., & Berry, L.L. (1990). Delivering Quality Service: Balancing Customer Perceptions and Expectations. New York: The Free Press.

Zomerdijk, L., & Voss, C.A. (2010). Service design for experience centric services. Journal of Service Research, 13(1), 67–82.

That's all Folks!